In my kitchen in Capri

With Mamma

Friends in the kitchen,
New Orleans

Nonna Regina and the
newest bambina

A juicy Redfish,
Plaquemines Parish

"Mangia!" in beautiful Capri

The family visits the restaurant

My Home is Your Home

My Home is Your Home

RECIPES FOR A HEALTHY, HAPPY LIFE
FROM 45 YEARS OF COOKING FOR FAMILY AND FRIENDS

by ANDREA APUZZO with JOHN DeMERS

PHOTOGRAPHS by KERRI McCAFFETY

Book and jacket design: Kerri McCaffety and Cynthia McCaffety

ISBN 978-0-9709336-7-6

Library of Congress Control Number: 2006930844

Printed in Korea.

Dillard's and Williams-Sonoma of New Orleans provided china,
pottery, silverware and linens for many of the pictured settings.

Published for Benvenuto Ltd. by

Vissi d'Arte Books
P. O. Box 791054
New Orleans, LA 70179

www.vissidartebooks.com

VISSI
D'ARTE

Contents

Lee Meriwether & Irma Thomas

The Judels

Joe Maselli

Ron & Allyson Bordelon

Tommy Lasorda

Foreword

by John DeMers

I'd like you to meet my friend, Andrea Apuzzo—whose home, within these pages, becomes our home.

What's that? You've already met him? Well, if you've dined at his restaurant Andrea's, it's a solid bet you have. For a chef who still cooks every day (unlike many of his peers, who spend their lives in offices signing papers on clipboards that cover every square inch of wall), Andrea manages to spend every day in his dining room as well. It's a bit of a mystery, a bit of a miracle—and the kind of contradiction you get used to, the more and better you get to know Andrea. Yes, he's there in his dining room, kissing ladies young and old, calling all little girls his "princesses," and sharing a glass of wine with the business leaders and politicos who try to keep New Orleans on its feet day after day. You might say Andrea is a politico himself, or at least that he lives like he's always running for office. Who knows, he may run for something some day. I'd vote for him. Louisiana has elected lots worse. Lots of times.

As a chef—meaning, with less ostentation, as a total food guy—Andrea is clearly the sum of all his parts: an upbringing on the isle of Capri, a career that began at a bakery when he was only seven, training and apprenticeships in grand hotels all over Europe, adventures in Bermuda and Atlanta, and his fateful pilgrimage to New Orleans. Through it all, he has stuck to what he knows best: terrific Italian food. Yet he has also embraced the Creole and Cajun cuisines of south Louisiana, letting them drift and drizzle through his culinary consciousness, offering a finessed ingredient here or an improved technique there. What this means is that, every bit as much as Andrea has cooked to please himself, he has cooked to please his customers. The fact that some of our favorite dishes at Andrea's are named after men and women who've been dining with this chef for three decades says a mouthful. Literally and figuratively.

I don't actually remember meeting Andrea, but I also don't remember not knowing him. In the news media, as in his dining room, Andrea makes sure he meets you. He met me shortly after I declared myself a food journalist 25 years ago, first in my hometown of New Orleans and later in 128 foreign countries. You could be crass and say he's just another of those headline-grabbing, media-mongering chefs. But having known not dozens but hundreds of headline-grabbing, media-mongering chefs, I'm here to promise you that would be missing the point. With Andrea, the point is that he is so single-minded in his pursuit—in his kitchen, in his dining room, on each and every plate—that his passion produces what is, for all the smiling faces, an essentially solitary life. Andrea is lonely for people who share his passion, some version of his mission and work ethic, some understanding of what all this achieves and how much it costs him each day. I am honored and grateful that he sees me as such a person.

A decade ago, when I was about to take a cruise that visited Naples for all of one day, I asked Andrea whether he'd recommend an excursion to the nearby ruins of Pompeii or a quick hydrofoil over to his isle of Capri. I figured he'd show his home-town pride, but might also offer some helpful insights into a place I'd never been. Instead, he sort of mumbled, "It doesn't matter." What? I was confused. Maybe a little hurt. I mean, what kind of answer was that?

"Well—" I responded eloquently.

"It doesn't matter," he said, "if you're only going to spend one day. Go wherever you like." He gazed down into his Chianti, then looked straight at me. "What you're supposed to do is go to Capri for days, maybe weeks, stay at my family's house and let my mother and my relatives show you around. That's when it matters what you choose to do."

I was thunderstruck.

I'd been, by this time, all over most corners of Europe, parts of Asia, much of Latin America, even to Australia and New Zealand. But not once had anyone offered to insert me into his culture and his family. Though it presented some interesting passport challenges and meant getting off the cruise ship for good in Naples, I accepted Andrea's invitation. I accepted the ride up to his village of Anacapri with a nephew I was sure any of my daughters would have fallen in love with. I let his mother, Regina, show me around the little house where I'd be staying. And most of all, I let Capri happen to me. Spending every waking hour walking up or down an incline made me feel healthier, younger and more alive within hours. Eating food based on olive oil, fresh seafood and glorious herbs, without any cream or butter in sight, made me clean my plate but shrink my waistline. And simply breathing in an island with thousands of years of history, where Homer's seductive sirens lured sailors onto the rocks, where

Roman emperors built summer homes, where many of Europe's most extravagant writers, painters, and musicians celebrated life and love among a year-round cascade of flowers, made me understand why I'd ever bothered to breathe in the first place.

Of course, for me, the question was overwhelming: How could Andrea ever leave such a place? The best answer had to wait even more years, until I sat down with Andrea for an in-depth magazine interview. No one could love Capri more than Andrea does, it seems. Yet, somewhat to my surprise, no one could love America more either. As I would struggle to express it, Capri remains home to Andrea, the center of his physical and emotional universe. But Capri, even now but certainly half a century ago, was still a piece of the Old World—that place of limited vision and limited opportunity, where what you died with was most likely what you had been born with. I can only imagine how the little boy who became Andrea grumbled about such claustrophobic horizons. Andrea, I'm guessing, wanted to create from the day he was born, wanted to build and acquire. You might say Andrea was born to embrace the American Dream, and embrace it he has.

As a person born in the twentieth century, I sometimes try to remind him that we Americans have our limitations too, that we as a people have our failures—we fail our nation, fail each other and fail our increasingly diverse collection of dreams. But Andrea, in his own way that is both exasperating and entrancing, won't hear a word of it. Like many Americans who've built buildings and bridges, dug highways and canals, raised great cities from the wilderness, and fought and died for freedom, Andrea is a patriot with an accent. And we who speak only standard American English have so very much to learn.

Writing this book with Andrea has been far more work than fun, despite frequent applications of Chianti to the cooks as well as to the cooking. Andrea, predictably, is quite the taskmaster, our kitchen sessions lasting eight, ten, or twelve hours if they lasted a minute. There were days and nights I wanted to stalk out, and presumably when Andrea wanted to as well. But we didn't. True to his life and his tradition and his food and his passion, we simply didn't. At the end of it all, I knew so much that was new yet also what I'd always known—that I really like this guy. Ultimately, it's hard not to like a man and his adopted country when both are constructed on the passionate living of dreams.

J. D.

Acknowledgments

With special thanks to my baking and pastry mentor, Massimino Maria Galardo Carmine of Anacapri, who gave me the opportunity to grow up as a kid so fast at the age of 7½ and who taught me like a father to be what I am today.

I would like to thank the staff of Andrea's Restaurant. I could not have done it without you. I would also like to give special thanks to all of my good friends and loyal guests for the past 22 years.

With many thanks to John DeMers for helping write this cookbook and to Kerri McCaffety for her brilliant photography. Many thanks also to Mr. and Mrs. Sidney Lassen for being so strong; to Michael and Jill Botnick, and to Mr. and Mrs. Henry Shane for all of your support. And to Ron Pincus, former general manager of the Royal Orleans Hotel, for encouraging me to open my home to others. I would like to thank my friends Eddie Gurret, corporate chef of the Princess Hotels, and Roland Mesnier, pastry chef of Princess Hotels.

All gratitude goes out to my uncle, Nello Romano, to Constantino, Roberto and the entire D'Angelis family for giving me the opportunity to open my home. I'd like to thank Claudio D'Angelo, who gave me the opportunity to come to America and make all of my dreams come true. To all of my friends and family all around the world, thank you from place to place: Switzerland, Bermuda, France, England, Argentina, Brazil, Mexico, Italy and Germany. I have been very lucky to meet so many wonderful people and friends to help my career.

Grazie di Tutti! Ciao!
Andrea

Welcome!

My home is your home. Or with the loveliness of my native Italian, I might say: *La mia casa e tua casa.* It is our special way of describing what it feels like to be embraced into our culture, our cuisine and our hospitality to strangers. In fact, as I hope you realize in the pages of this book, there really *are* no strangers. Food and wine connect us to each other—and also to what I call the "happy, healthy life." The recipes in this book are not about eating light; they are about eating *right*—living an entire life based on variety and moderation, then letting that life be the example for how we cook and eat. These foods, generally, are what I consider healthy—constructed around fresh, seasonal and hopefully local ingredients, enjoyed in portions appropriate to our life-styles, and most importantly, shared with the people we love. The dishes produced by these recipes, in other words, will continually strike you as the exact opposite of the way too many of us eat in America today.

We wolf down far too many meals alone, something the Mediterranean world would consider strange and probably dangerous. We eat far too many meals in a hurry, sometimes when we really have to but, with amazing regularity, when we only *presume* we have to. And quite frankly, we eat far too many of our meals in portions far too large—a function of eating until we're satisfied by an experience never *designed* to satisfy. It is a truth of the Old World we could use in the New: people who enjoy good food and wine with enough time, family and friends almost never feel the need to overeat. It is a dark irony that here in America, where we long looked disapprovingly at cultures who approached mealtimes with gusto, we now are more obese as a nation than those people ever were. It makes you think. Or it *should* make you think. And as an Italian who truly loves America and its people, these pages can never be about having the last laugh. They must always be about finding ways to eat and drink that give us many more years of laughter. I invite you to join me on the journey.

As you have gathered by now, I am a chef. I've been involved in the loving preparation of food since I went to work at a bakery down the street from my village on the isle of Capri—when I was seven years old. Ever earlier than that, however, I was aware of the passionate transaction that occurs anytime someone cooks for others with love. I saw it most clearly in the labors applied by my mother, and indeed by all the mothers of our village, growing and harvesting fresh produce on the rugged hillsides of our island and disappearing into our small kitchens to make magic happen. Capri, of course, has always been described as magical—often by the British and Northern European writers who adopted my island as their escape from cold and gray. Yet as much as I appreciate the "good press" Capri has received from people in love with the written word, I've always believed our true magic was in those simple daily acts of giving that happened in my mother's kitchen. It was as though we all understood this, even that we all took it for granted, each time we sat down with our close family and extended family for even the least extravagant meals of freshness, flavor and life-long affection. That's a lot to serve on a single dinner plate. But however my mother described what she had cooked for us, that's *always* what she was serving.

For all you've heard about the pressures of the restaurant business, this is what I've tried to serve on every plate at Andrea's since the day we opened our doors. Coming to New Orleans in 1977, I felt immediately that I'd stumbled into a world of kindred spirits. Yes, I came here for a job—to serve as chef at the venerable Royal Orleans Hotel—and at some level I suspected I might soon move on. It is what chefs do—the primary way we advance our culinary careers. Yet suspicion that I might *get* to move on evolved quickly into fear that I might *have* to move on, and then into determination that I wasn't moving. It's a determination many native New Orleanians know well; still, for a guy from Capri to feel he'd found his home here might strike you as strange. Happily, my embrace of New Orleans, its culture and its people has been anything but one-sided. To this day, I have customers at Andrea's who started eating my cooking at the Royal Orleans. And nearly every day I meet someone in my dining room whose parents—or yes, even grandparents—told them they had to come here, order this or that house specialty and ask to meet the chef. Feeling this gratitude forms one of the most satisfying aspects of a life devoted to food and wine.

Before we head from here to the place I feel most at home—the kitchen, naturally, with you right at my elbow—I should tell you two things this book is *not.* In the typical sense, it is not a chef's cookbook. You know the kind I mean; in fact, to some degree, my very first cookbook *was* one. It's not so much that those earlier recipes are difficult, since many, many novice home cooks have learned to make great dishes from that book. It *is* that they are organized around classic sauces and techniques, whether specifically Italian, traditionally French, or belonging to the combined body of knowledge that is the trained chef's stock and trade. This book is different. We have tried on every page to reflect the way real people cook in their real home kitchens, offering sometimes a better way to do things but recognizing throughout the realities of equipment, expertise and time that bear down hard on any home cook. So follow the recipes in this book. They will work, and they will be wonderful. But follow them just far enough to realize you don't always have the follow them. It gives me the greatest pleasure and pride when my recipe is only the beginning of a dish you can someday call your own.

The second thing this is not is a "diet" or "light" cookbook, partially because I've already written one of those, too. The dynamic of such a book is to convince you, seemingly in conflict with your life experience, that you really *can* eat well and lose weight, lower your cholesterol, or whatever. It is a sad fact of American life that diets seldom work and tend to be followed for relatively short periods of time. Some books even boast of that fact, promising this or that shining result in as little as seven days. This is the *opposite* of that kind of book as well. In these pages, you will never encounter any form of self-deprivation or self-denial, never be told of some substitution that tastes almost as good as the "real thing." We suppose there's a place for books like that, but at this stage in our lives we have no interest in writing one. Quite simply: everything in this book IS the real thing. Made with quality. Made with care. And made with love.

My promise to you is as uncomplicated as life in an earlier time and, at least when we sit down for a meal, a better place. There will always be something simple and delicious on the stove, even when you drop by unexpectedly. There will always be a flavorful, rustic bottle of wine to be opened and shared. And there will always be that deep sense of welcome meant to say that, at this time and for as long as we're together, there's no place else you need or want to be. That's what the famous words mean, when you think about them. And that's why I always say: My home is your home!

Andrea Apuzzo
New Orleans
November 2006

Antipasti

Bruschetta Napolitana

In recent years, we in the United States have finally caught on to one of the most delightful starters or party hors d'oeuvres that, of course, the Italians have been doing for centuries. There's just something about the cool, fresh tomato topping when it's spooned onto grilled rustic bread. At Andrea's, this is often the first bite of food diners lift to their mouths—hunger being another good way to make sure they're properly appreciative.

For the Topping:

4 Roma tomatoes, chopped in small cubes
¼ cup finely chopped white onion
1 teaspoon minced garlic
⅓ cup extra-virgin olive oil
1 tablespoon chopped fresh basil
1 tablespoon chopped fresh oregano
¼ teaspoon salt

In a bowl, combine the tomatoes with the onion, garlic, olive oil, basil, oregano and salt. Let sit for 30-40 minutes to let flavors combine.

For the Bread:

½ cup pure olive oil
1 teaspoon minced garlic
Rustic Italian bread, preferably 1-2 days old, sliced ⅓" thick
Fresh basil leaves, cut in thin strips
Extra-virgin olive oil
4 slices Asiago or Provolone Cheese

Combine the olive oil and garlic in another bowl and spread generously over both sides of the bread. Grill on a preheated grill until marked on both sides. Set bread on plates or platters and cover with the tomato topping. Top with cheese slices and melt under a preheated broiler. Garnish with basil strips and a drizzle of additional olive oil. Serves 4.

Note: The tomato topping for bruschetta isn't just for bruschetta. Made exactly this way (or perhaps enhanced with things like capers or chopped red onions), you can spoon this luscious and colorful mixture over the top of grilled fish—or include it as the main component in a tomato vinaigrette for a toss of fresh greens. You'll probably start making double or even triple this recipe, as you find more and more ways to enjoy it!

Involtini di Melanzane Caruso

One of the best things about the eggplant "roll-up" antipasto is the tomato-basil sauce that gives it life. At Andrea's, as at your home, you can make enough of this sauce to feed the multitudes, since that is surely what you'll end up doing. It's great spooned over chicken or fish. Or tossed with some nice pasta, it's a natural in more ways than one.

Tomato-Basil Sauce:
½ cup pure olive oil
¼ cup finely chopped onion
2 teaspoons minced garlic
½ cup red wine
4 cups canned Italian plum tomatoes
4 cups juice from tomatoes
1 teaspoon salt
¼ teaspoon ground white pepper
4 sprigs fresh oregano, chopped
16 fresh basil leaves, chopped
8 sprigs Italian parsley, chopped
2 bay leaves

Prepare the sauce by heating the olive oil in a large pan and sautéing the onion and garlic until they are transparent. Add the wine and bring to a boil, followed by the tomatoes, squeezing them between your fingers. Add the tomato juice, lower heat, and simmer for about 30 minutes. Add the salt, pepper, oregano, basil, parsley and bay leaves. Simmer for 15-20 minutes.

1 eggplant, thinly sliced lengthwise (14 slices) and sprinkled with salt
½ cup pure olive oil
1 pound fresh buffalo mozzarella, sliced, then cut into sticks
12 large leaves fresh basil

Sauté the eggplant slices in batches in the olive oil until golden brown, 2 to 3 minutes per side. Drain on paper towels. Set out the eggplant slices on a clean, flat surface and top each with a basil leaf and then a stick of mozzarella. Roll the eggplant around the filling. Cover the bottom of a large casserole or baking dish with the tomato-basil sauce. Arrange the eggplant roll-ups on top of the sauce. Bake the roll-ups in a preheated 425° oven long enough to melt the cheese, 8-10 minutes.

Fresh basil leaves
Grated Parmesan cheese

Meanwhile, decorate appetizer plates with fresh basil leaves. Remove the baking dish from the oven and let rest for 5 minutes. Serve 2 roll-ups on each plate, sprinkled with Parmesan cheese. Serves 6-8.

Marinated Artichokes Orsola

Here's a wonderful antipasto that everybody loves in New Orleans, since artichoke is one of those foods that arrived here with Italian immigrants and quickly found favor with all locals. Today, it might be considered a "New Orleans food," but I'm delighted to tell you this recipe will remind you where it came from.

1 gallon water *Juice of 1 lemon* *¼ cup salt* *⅓ cup white vinegar*	Bring the water to a boil with the lemon juice, salt and vinegar.
4 whole artichokes	Meanwhile, trim the hard, sharp ends off the artichokes. Slice them down the middle, scoop out the furry choke and cut each half into four wedges. Put these wedges in the boiling water and cook until tender. Drain and cool.
2 cups extra-virgin olive oil *3 cups pure olive oil* *2 tablespoons minced garlic* *3 bay leaves* *½ teaspoon crushed red pepper* *1 teaspoon salt* *1 teaspoon crushed dry oregano*	Transfer the artichokes to a baking dish and mix with the olive oils, garlic, bay leaves, red pepper, salt and oregano. Marinate in the refrigerator for at least 3 hours before serving on a platter. Serves 6-8.

Note: This same recipe can be prepared with baby artichokes or with only the artichoke hearts.

My Grandmother's Stuffed Artichokes

Any dish that I name after my grandmother—presumably like any dish you name after yours—inhabits a special place in our hearts and in our kitchens. I remember watching her make this dish for us back home in Capri, each step carried out with simplicity and so much love. If you want to keep your guests chattering happily around your table of antipasti, I promise this recipe will hit a homerun.

4 artichokes, cleaned
Water with ⅓ cup lemon juice

Clean the artichokes by trimming off the spiny, hard leaves on the outside, then pulling them open from the top to scoop out the furry choke within. Set in water mixed with lemon juice to prevent discoloration.

Stuffing:

2 cups unseasoned bread crumbs
1 cup Parmesan or Romano cheese (or mixed)
¼ cup chopped fresh oregano
¼ cup finely chopped fresh basil
8 anchovy fillets in oil, plus
¼ cup of the oil
¼ teaspoon crushed red pepper
1 tablespoon minced garlic
2 tablespoons finely chopped onion
½ cup extra-virgin olive oil
⅓ cup pure olive oil
¼ cup chopped Italian parsley
¼ teaspoon salt
¼ teaspoon black pepper

Prepare the stuffing by mixing all ingredients in a large bowl with your fingers until the breadcrumbs are moist. Press the stuffing into the space behind each leaf and down into the hollowed-out center of each artichoke.

1 cup white wine
5 cups water
¼ cup pure olive oil

Set the artichokes in a baking pan with the wine and water. Drizzle with the olive oil. Transfer to a preheated 400° oven for 45 minutes, until the tops are golden brown.

Topping:

1 cup extra-virgin olive oil
1 tablespoon minced garlic
1 tablespoon chopped fresh Italian parsley
1 teaspoon finely chopped green onion
⅛ teaspoon salt
⅛ teaspoon black pepper
Juice of 1 lemon

Meanwhile, prepare the topping by mixing all ingredients in a bowl. Topping can be sprinkled over top of artichokes or put in a decorative bowl for dipping. Serves 6-8.

Lobster Martini

Anything served in a martini glass these days is called a martini—even when it wanders far from the original American cocktail. This antipasto takes the basic plan out of the bar and into your kitchen. With the expansion of seafood counters that will steam your lobsters while you wait, it just got lots easier to make at home as well.

1 gallon water
1 carrot, chopped
1 onion, chopped
1 stalk celery, chopped
3 bay leaves
3 cloves garlic
½ lemon
1 medium live lobster

Heat the water in a stock pot with the carrot, onion, celery, bay leaves, garlic and lemon. When it reaches a rolling boil, add the lobster and return to a boil. Cook 8 minutes, until lobster is bright red. Cool quickly by transferring to a tray of ice water. Break the cooked lobster into pieces, using heavy kitchen shears to cut the shell. Be careful to preserve the shape of the tail and claw meat (you can leave a piece of the tail shell for decoration). Clean and slice the head for garnish.

Dressing:
3 tablespoons prepared mayonnaise
1 tablespoon ketchup
2 tablespoons Ketel One vodka
4 drops Tabasco pepper sauce
⅛ teaspoon salt
⅛ teaspoon black pepper
Juice of ½ lemon
2 drops Worcestershire sauce

Whisk all ingredients together in a bowl.

1 Belgian endive
Mixed baby greens
Lemon slices for garnish

Remove the endive leaves and wash them under cold water. Position them in 2 large martini glasses, then fill with baby greens. Top the greens with lobster meat, with a cleaned and trimmed piece of shell for decoration. Spoon about 2 tablespoons of dressing over the top. Serve garnished with lemon slices. Serves 2.

Note: The seasoned water used here to boil lobster is also great for crawfish or crabs.

Crabmeat Stuffed Eggs Michael

Everybody loves stuffed hard-boiled eggs, especially the kind some people call "deviled." We borrow pages from several delicious books to give our guests these glorious celebrations of the Gulf's bounty, wrapped up in as much nostalgia as our memories of a childhood Fourth of July.

1 gallon salted water
¼ cup white vinegar
12 eggs

Bring the salted water to a boil with the vinegar. Cook the eggs in the boiling water 10-12 minutes, until hard-boiled, then cool by running under cold water.

½ teaspoon salt
½ teaspoon black pepper
3 tablespoons prepared mayonnaise
½ teaspoon Worcestershire sauce
¼ teaspoon Tabasco pepper sauce
Juice of 1 lemon
½ cup jumbo lump crabmeat
Louisiana choupique or Beluga caviar (optional)

Peel the eggs and slice each in half. Remove the yolks to a mixing bowl and whisk in the salt, pepper, mayonnaise, Worcestershire, Tabasco and lemon juice. Gently fold in the crabmeat. Use this mixture to fill the hard-boiled egg whites. Top with choupique or other caviar, if desired.

Romaine lettuce leaves
Lemon quarters
Chopped Italian parsley

Set the stuffed eggs on a platter atop leaves of Romaine. Garnish with lemon quarters and Italian parsley. Serves 8-10.

Ricchi e Poveri

For purposes of this salad with a rich cultural background, eating beans is for the poor and eating seafood is for the rich. Forget for the moment that both can be delicious. Thus, this mixture of beans and lightly poached calamari has picked up the tongue-in-cheek name—Rich and Poor.

2 cups cleaned and chopped calamari
2 quarts water
1 tablespoon salt
2-3 tablespoons white wine vinegar

Poach the calamari in salted water with a little white wine vinegar, bringing to a boil and then cooling rapidly in an ice bath.

1 cup cooked cannellini beans
1 stalk celery, with leaves, finely chopped
⅓ cup extra-virgin olive oil
1 teaspoon minced garlic
1 tablespoon finely chopped white onion
⅓ cup white wine
Juice of 1 lemon
½ teaspoon crushed red pepper
½ teaspoon Worcestershire sauce
⅛ teaspoon salt

Combine the cooled calamari with the beans and all remaining ingredients, tossing to mix well.

1 cup mixed baby greens
Lemon wedges for garnish

Divide the mixed greens over salad plates and top with the Rich and Poor Salad. Garnish with lemon wedges and, if desired, lemon-infused extra-virgin olive oil. Serves 4.

Zucchini alla Griglia Gelsomina

Though this dish can be prepared just fine in a sauté pan, I'm more than a little partial to the extra flavor added by that light charring provided by a grill. Either way, I think you and your guests will agree this is a terrific antipasto. And you'll probably find yourselves enjoying this dressing on just about everything, from grilled fish to the plainest grilled chicken breast!

2 medium zucchini, sliced and lightly coated with pure olive oil

Dressing:
1 tablespoon extra-virgin olive oil
1 tablespoon pure olive oil
1 tablespoon finely chopped white onion
½ teaspoon minced garlic
½ teaspoon chopped fresh Italian parsley
½ teaspoon chopped fresh oregano
½ teaspoon chopped fresh basil
¼ teaspoon crushed red pepper
¼ teaspoon salt
¼ teaspoon black pepper
1 tablespoon white vinegar
1 tablespoon white wine

Grill the zucchini slices on a preheated grill for only 3-5 minutes, turning once for even charring.

Mix the dressing in a bowl. Transfer the grilled zucchini to a platter and spoon the dressing over the top, coating each slice thoroughly. Serves 4-6.

Eggplant Caponatina Carmelina

The eggplant mix or relish known as caponata has gotten a bit better known in recent years, so I thought it was high time to add a twist or two. It's the capers and balsamic vinegar that give this variation its extra zing.

1 medium eggplant, sliced and cubed
¼ cup salt
1 cup vegetable oil

Cover the cubed eggplant with salt and set in a strainer. Place a weight on top to press bitter liquids into a bowl under the strainer. Discard the liquid. In a sauté pan, heat the vegetable oil and fry the cubed eggplant in batches, being careful not to overcrowd. Drain on paper towels.

½ cup pure olive oil
½ cup finely chopped white onion
1 tablespoon minced garlic
1 cup canned crushed tomatoes with juice
10 cherry tomatoes
¼ cup balsamic vinegar
2 tablespoons chopped fresh basil
1 tablespoon chopped fresh oregano
¼ cup capers
½ teaspoon salt
½ teaspoon crushed red pepper

In a separate large pan, heat the olive oil and caramelize the onion and garlic. Add the crushed tomatoes, then hand-crush the cherry tomatoes and add. Stir in the balsamic vinegar and all remaining ingredients. Bring to a boil, then reduce heat and simmer about 3 minutes. Stir in the fried eggplant and let cool. Serve on a platter. Serves 4-6.

Roasted Garlic Henry Shane

Happily, it's become fairly commonplace in Italian restaurants across America to be served a bowl for olive oil along with some hot, crusty bread almost as soon as you sit down. Some of the better waiters will even whip up their own "special" olive oil right before your eyes. Once you prepare this recipe even once, you'll have a lot higher standards about where your bread goes a-dipping.

1 cup whole garlic cloves
1 cup pure olive oil
½ teaspoon crushed red pepper
¼ teaspoon salt
½ teaspoon chopped fresh rosemary
½ teaspoon chopped fresh Italian parsley

Pan-roast the garlic cloves with the olive oil in an ovenproof skillet, cooking till the cloves are golden and sweetly caramelized. Add the crushed red pepper and transfer the skillet to a preheated 400° oven for 4-5 minutes, just until the garlic is soft. Pour the garlic and oil onto a platter and mix in the salt, rosemary and parsley. Let stand 10-15 minutes for flavors to combine, then serve with slices of grilled or toasted rustic bread. Serves 6-8.

Eggplant Parmigiana Panini

As more and more Americans have come to understand, panini are Italian sandwiches—sometimes just rolls stuffed with wonderful cold cuts and cheeses, other times toasted or (even better) grilled. But … even better than those, I think, is this wild idea I had for taking my beloved tomato and fresh mozzarella and "sandwiching" them between slices of fried eggplant. These panini will disappear quickly, so you might want to make a lot of them.

1 medium eggplant
1 cup all-purpose flour
2 eggs beaten
2 cups unseasoned breadcrumbs
Salt and black pepper

Slice the eggplant into 8 rounds. Prepare 3 side-by-side platters of flour, eggs and breadcrumbs, seasoning each with salt and pepper. Move the eggplant rounds through in that order, coating thoroughly.

½ cup vegetable oil

Fry till golden brown in vegetable oil. Drain on paper towels.

4 tablespoons pure olive oil
4 thick slices beefsteak tomato

Heat the olive oil in a separate sauté pan and cook the tomato slices very fast on both sides, flecking with brown.

4 thick slices fresh mozzarella
1 tablespoon chopped fresh basil
1 tablespoon chopped fresh oregano
¼ cup grated Parmesan cheese
Fresh basil leaves

Make a stack of the sautéed tomatoes and mozzarella slices, with the chopped herbs and Parmesan in between and on the top. Set 4 eggplant slices on a baking sheet, top with tomato and mozzarella stack, then with another eggplant round. Sprinkle with Parmesan and set in a preheated 350° oven until cheese starts to melt, about 5 minutes. Slice in half and serve on platter garnished with basil leaves. Serves 4-6.

Polpette di Melanzane Nello

Have you ever wanted meatballs but just didn't want any meat?—I know, me neither! But I promise you'll love these meatless "meatballs" anyway. And hey, in New Orleans, where we still take the pre-Easter Lenten season pretty seriously, this dish, named after my uncle who helped me open Andrea's, just might be the answer to a whole lot of fervent prayers.

2 medium eggplants
1 cup water

Slice the eggplants in half and score the insides with a sharp knife. Place them cut side-down in a roasting pan with the water and roast in a preheated 425° oven until tender, about 25 minutes.

½ cup pure olive oil
2 tablespoons finely chopped white onion
1 tablespoon minced garlic
1 stalk celery, finely chopped
12 sprigs fresh Italian parsley, finely chopped
6 leaves fresh basil, finely chopped
1 tablespoon chopped fresh oregano

Meanwhile, heat the olive oil and caramelize the onion, garlic and celery until golden, then stir in the parsley, basil and oregano.

8 slices white bread
1½ cups whole milk

In a bowl, crumble the bread and combine with the milk.

1½ cups breadcrumbs
½ cup grated Parmesan cheese
1 egg, beaten
½ teaspoon salt
¼ teaspoon black pepper

Scoop out the flesh from the cooled eggplant and chop it finely, or purée in a food processor. Combine the puréed eggplant with the sautéed vegetables and heat until thoroughly incorporated. Turn off heat and mix in the breadcrumbs and the Parmesan. Squeeze the excess milk from the crumbled bread and add it to the eggplant mixture. Add the egg. Season with salt and pepper. Refrigerate for 10 minutes to make the mixture easier to handle.

1 cup all-purpose flour
3 eggs, beaten
1 cup unseasoned breadcrumbs
Vegetable oil for frying
Marinara Sauce
Chopped fresh Italian parsley

Line up three platters, one each for the flour, the eggs, and the breadcrumbs. Roll the eggplant mixture into about 36 tablespoon-sized balls and place them on wax paper. Dip each ball into the flour, the eggs, and then the breadcrumbs, coating thoroughly. Deep (or skillet) fry at 375° until golden brown. Drain on paper towels. Serve on a platter with marinara sauce, garnished with Italian parsley. Serves 8-10.

Prosciutto di Parma e Fiche

One of the simplest primi piatti we can think of is actually one of the best. It's the perfect way to start practically any meal when figs are in season. The lemon-infused olive oil from Sorrento supplies the perfect accent. This is a terrific buffet item.

¼ pound fresh buffalo mozzarella, sliced
16 figs, sliced open
16 thin slices prosciutto di Parma
Lemon-infused olive oil
8 fresh basil leaves for garnish

Layer the figs on salad plates with the slices of mozzarella, 2 slices per person. Drizzle with the lemon oil. Garnish with fresh basil. Serves 4.

Arancini di Riso Grelletta Sr.

The name of this antipasto is strictly visual—the words "little oranges" referring to the shape rather than any real relationship to citrus fruit. Though today a popular antipasto item, arancini often drag native Italians back to their earliest memories of train and bus stations. It's the sort of food you can eat on the run, during those brief whistle stops on transport that goes from rustic village to rustic village.

2 tablespoons pure olive oil
1 tablespoon finely chopped white onion
1 teaspoon minced garlic
1 cup Arborio rice
2 cups water or stock
1 teaspoon salt
½ teaspoon white pepper
1 bay leaf

Heat the olive oil in an ovenproof pot and lightly brown the onion and garlic. Pour in the rice and stir to coat, then pour in the water or stock along with the salt, white pepper and bay leaf. Bring to a boil, then set the pot uncovered in a preheated 400° oven until the rice is tender and all liquid is absorbed, 10-12 minutes. Let the rice cool.

10 slices salami, chopped
5 slices mortadella, chopped
1 slice prosciutto, chopped
½ cup grated Parmesan cheese
1 tablespoon minced garlic
1 tablespoon finely chopped onion
½ teaspoon ground nutmeg
½ teaspoon salt
½ teaspoon black pepper
1 tablespoon chopped fresh Italian parsley
1 tablespoon chopped fresh basil
1 tablespoon chopped fresh oregano
½ teaspoon crushed red pepper
⅓ cup fresh or frozen green peas

In a large bowl, combine the chopped meats with the cooled rice. Mix in all remaining ingredients through the green peas.

1 cup all-purpose flour
2 eggs, beaten
1 cup unseasoned breadcrumbs
Vegetable oil for frying
Chopped fresh basil
Tomato-Basil Sauce (recipe p. 21)

Line up three platters side by side with the flour, the beaten eggs and the breadcrumbs. Form the mixture into arancini about the size of golf balls (makes 14-16) and move them from platter to platter, coating thoroughly. Fry in batches in vegetable oil until golden brown and drain on paper towels. Serve on a platter garnished with chopped basil. Excellent with Tomato-Basil Sauce for dipping. Serves 6-8.

Boccancini di Salmon

I love smoked salmon served just about any way you can serve it, and sometimes the simpler the better. Still, here's a nice antipasto called "little bites" that will strike your guests as a lot harder to make than it really is. It takes a bit of time but you can do the preparation in advance and keep the results in the freezer, all set for quick slicing, assembling on toast and serving.

8 thin slices smoked salmon
1 cup baby spinach leaves

Lay the salmon slices overlapping slightly on plastic wrap. Wilt the spinach leaves in boiling water for 1 minute, then drain and pat dry. Arrange the spinach leaves evenly on the salmon.

2 tablespoons dairy sour cream
½ cup cream cheese
3 sprigs fresh dill, chopped
¼ teaspoon Tabasco pepper sauce
½ teaspoon Worcestershire sauce
½ teaspoon minced garlic

Combine in a mixing bowl to form a thick spread.

4-5 slices roasted red bell pepper

Spread the cheese filling over the salmon and spinach, then top with the red bell peppers. Carefully grasp the near edge of the plastic wrap and roll the filled salmon lengthwise, using a rubber spatula to press the roll tightly. Twist the ends of the wrap closed and place in the freezer until 10-15 minutes before serving.

Toasted rounds of whole wheat bread

Slice the salmon roll and serve on whole-wheat toast rounds. Makes about 20.

Frutti di Mare Portofino

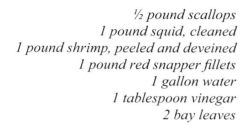

Sometimes you see mixed seafood dishes like this done in the oven with lots of butter and cheese, and served piping hot. In French, some menus call this dish *fruits de mer.* The same basic name finds its way into Italian, not surprisingly, as a much fresher and much lighter creation, perfect for the coast of Italy—or the coast of Louisiana.

½ pound scallops
1 pound squid, cleaned
1 pound shrimp, peeled and deveined
1 pound red snapper fillets
1 gallon water
1 tablespoon vinegar
2 bay leaves

Wash all the seafood. Combine the water, vinegar and bay leaves and bring to a boil. With a slotted spoon, add the scallops to the water and poach for 5 minutes, or until water returns to a boil. Remove and repeat with the squid, shrimp, and snapper. Drain and refrigerate the seafood.

1½ pounds mussels, in shell
1½ pounds clams, in shell
¼ cup extra virgin olive oil
2 teaspoons chopped onions
1 teaspoon chopped garlic
¼ teaspoon crushed red pepper
½ teaspoon salt
¼ teaspoon white pepper
½ cup dry white wine

Heat the ¼ cup of olive oil in a large skillet until very hot. Saute the onions and garlic until lightly browned. Add crushed red pepper, salt and pepper. Put the mussels into the pan and add the wine. Bring the wine to a boil, reduce heat, and cover the pan. Cook the mussels until they open, about 5 minutes. Remove mussels from the pan and repeat the procedure with the clams. Refrigerate the mussels and clams until cold. Remove about half of the clams and mussels from shells and chop them coarsely.

½ pound lump crabmeat, chilled

When all the seafood is chilled, remove from the refrigerator along with the chilled crabmeat.

Sauce:
I cup extra-virgin olive oil
¼ cup lemon juice
½ cup dry white wine
1½ teaspoons Worcestershire
¼ cup chopped Italian parsley
1½ teaspoons chopped garlic
2 teaspoons chopped onion
Romaine or Bibb letuce

Whisk together all the sauce ingredients in a large bowl. Add all the seafoods and toss lightly. Serve atop the lettuce and surround with the mussels and clams in the shells. Serves 6.

Creole Shrimp Cocktail

Everybody makes shrimp cocktail—mainly because everybody loves shrimp cocktail. I decided to do the job a little better, combining some of my favorite flavors from all the years I've spent in New Orleans. And no, that doesn't mean it'll burn your mouth off—I hate it when that's all people *think* they know about New Orleans cooking.

1 gallon water
1 carrot, chopped
1 onion, chopped
1 stalk celery, chopped
3 bay leaves
3 cloves garlic
½ lemon
8 sprigs fresh dill
Wild baby greens
Lemon slices
24 (21/25 size) shrimp

Boil the water with the vegetables, herbs and lemon, then add the shrimp. Cook just until water returns to a boil, then cool the shrimp quickly in an ice-water bath to prevent overcooking. Peel the shrimp, leaving only the tail.

Sauce:

3 tablespoons prepared mayonnaise
1 tablespoon prepared horseradish
2 tablespoons prepared chili sauce
1 tablespoon chopped green onion
1 teaspoon minced garlic
1 teaspoon Worcestershire sauce
½ teaspoon Tabasco pepper sauce
1 tablespoon New Orleans rum
1 teaspoon finely chopped fresh dill
¼ teaspoon salt
⅛ teaspoon pepper

Prepare the sauce by combining all ingredients in a bowl. Serve the shrimp atop wild baby greens on a platter, with lemon slices for garnish. You can spoon the sauce over the top or serve it in a bowl on the side. Serves 4.

Marina Grande, Capri

Calamari with Lentils and Escarole

A lot of Americans have learned to love calamari in recent years, though I'm always happy when I can gently nudge someone beyond the standard-issue batter-fried with marinara sauce. Here is a great antipasto that a lot of my guests love, one that I think is purer in terms of calamari's taste and texture than its fried brethren everywhere. The lentils and escarole offer a very nice contrast.

1 cup dry lentils
1½ cups water
1 stalk celery, finely chopped
2 bay leaves

Cook the lentils until tender in the water with the celery and bay leaves.

2 tablespoons pure olive oil
2 tablespoons finely chopped white onion
1 tablespoon minced garlic
½ pound sliced calamari
½ cup white wine
Juice of 1 lemon

In a separate pan, heat the 2 tablespoons olive oil and caramelize the onion and garlic. Add the calamari, stir briefly, then pour in the wine and lemon juice. Bring to a boil, reduce heat and simmer.

2 heads escarole, washed and roughly chopped
1 tablespoon pure olive oil
1 teaspoon crushed red pepper
Extra-virgin olive oil

In another pan, quickly wilt the escarole in the remaining olive oil. Pour in ½ cup of the cooking liquid from the lentils. Add the crushed red pepper and cook just until escarole is dark green, 5-7 minutes. Drain the cooked lentils, reserving the stock for vegetable soup. Mix the lentils with the calamari and escarole. Season to taste with salt and pepper. Let cool. Serve on a platter drizzled with extra-virgin olive oil. Serves 6-8.

Primi Piatti

Gamberi Catarina

This classic dish is named in honor of the great Di Medici, the force behind so much that was wonderful in Italy during the Renaissance. In our case. It's also named after shrimp, the force behind so much that is wonderful in New Orleans cooking.

$^1/_3$ cup extra-virgin olive oil
2 tablespoons chopped white onion
1 tablespoon minced garlic
2 tablespoons chopped leek, green and white parts
$^1/_4$ teaspoon crushed red pepper
36 medium shrimp, peeled and deveined
$^1/_4$ cup brandy
$^1/_2$ cup white wine
$^1/_4$ cup freshly squeezed lemon juice
1 cup fish or shrimp stock
1 tablespoon chopped fresh oregano
1 tablespoon chopped fresh basil
1 teaspoon chopped fresh rosemary leaves
$^1/_4$ teaspoon salt
1 teaspoon Worcestershire sauce

Heat the oil in a large pan and sauté the onion and garlic until caramelized. Stir in the leek and red pepper, sautéing briefly. Add the shrimp and stir over high heat just until pink. Flame with the brandy, then add the wine, lemon juice and stock. Remove the shrimp, leaving the liquid. Reduce the liquid over high heat, then add the oregano, basil, rosemary, salt and Worcestershire.

2 tablespoons unsalted butter
$^1/_4$ cup grated Parmesan cheese
$^1/_4$ cup unseasoned breadcrumbs
Lemon wedges

Return the shrimp to the pan. Add the butter, stirring until incorporated. Remove the pan from the heat and stir in the cheese and the breadcrumbs. Divide over large appetizer plates. Garnish with lemon wedges. Serves 4.

Gamberi al Barbecue Nola

By now, most people know that New Orleans-style barbecue shrimp have nothing to do with "barbecuing" and everything to do with the city's rich Italian heritage. We've taken the basic New Orleans idea and added some flavorful touches of our own.

2 tablespoons pure olive oil
4 garlic cloves, minced
14 jumbo shrimp, heads on
2 teaspoons chopped fresh rosemary leaves
½ teaspoon crushed red pepper
2 teaspoons paprika
½ cup dry white wine
1 teaspoon chopped fresh basil
1 teaspoon chopped fresh oregano
4 tablespoons shrimp stock
4 bay leaves, crushed

Heat the oil in a sauté pan and sauté the garlic until caramelized. Add the shrimp, rosemary, red pepper and paprika, cooking until the shrimp just turn pink. Add the wine and cook until absorbed, then add all remaining ingredients. Bring to a boil, then lower heat to a simmer and cook for 7 minutes. Serves 2.

Eggplant Crabcakes Andrea

I always loved crabcakes, but I always thought they were missing something—until I started bringing eggplant into the picture. It gives the dish another wonderful taste and texture, and it simply seems more Italian. No wonder I like it so much!

2 whole eggplants
1 teaspoon salt
1 cup water

Preheat oven to 400°. Cut eggplants in half lengthwise. Place in a baking pan, sprinkle with salt, and add water. Bake 30 minutes or until tender.

1 white onion, chopped
2 ounces garlic, chopped
2 tablespoons pure olive oil
6 celery sticks, finely diced
1 medium sized leek, chopped
1 tablespoon thyme
1 tablespoon marjoram
3 ounces white wine

Sauté the onion and garlic in the olive oil until golden brown. Add celery, leek, herbs and wine and mix well. Place in a food processor with the meat of the baked eggplants, which has been scooped out with a spoon. Mix well and set aside.

1 tablespoon pure olive oil
2 pounds crabmeat
2 ounces white wine
½ teaspoon salt
¼ teaspoon black pepper
1 teaspoon peperoncino
1 cup bread crumbs
½ cup grated Parmesan cheese
1 tablespoon pure olive oil

Place the oil, crabmeat and wine in another skillet and bring to a boil. Add the salt, pepper, peperoncino and the eggplant mixture. Mix well and allow to cool. Spoon into a bowl and combine with the bread crumbs and Parmesan. Form into patties of about 4 ounces each. Coat each side lightly with additional bread crumbs and sauté in olive oil until golden brown on both sides.

2 ounces meunier sauce
Green scallions for garnish

Serve on a plate topped with the remaining crabmeat. Add 2 ounces of meunier sauce and garnish with green scallions. Serves 4.

Beef Carpaccio

My guests love this modern classic, created at Harry's Bar in Venice in the golden days when Papa Hemingway was a regular there and Cipriani still ran the bar before he started his own luxury hotel reached by elegant launch from the Piazza San Marco. That's the good life this dish evokes!

8 (3-ounce) slices filet mignon	Place the filets between plastic wrap and pound them out with a mallet until they're about 8 inches across and very thin.
½ cup mayonnaise *3 tablespoons Italian Senape (or Dijon) mustard* *½ teaspoon Tabasco pepper sauce* *½ teaspoon Worcestershire sauce* *2 tablespoons brandy* *4 tablespoons whipping cream* *½ teaspoon freshly squeezed lemon juice* *Extra-virgin olive oil* *1 lemon, quartered*	Whisk together the mayonnaise, mustard, Tabasco, Worcestershire, brandy, whipping cream and lemon juice. Lightly coat the beef with the olive oil, then squeeze on the juice from a lemon quarter.
Shaved Parmesan cheese *2 small mushrooms, sliced* *1 lemon, quartered*	Serve on plates topped with the sauce. Garnish with remaining lemon, shaved Parmesan, and mushroom slices. Serves 2.

Tuna Carpaccio

Even though the beef carpaccio was created at Harry's Bar first, this version made with fresh tuna has somewhat overtaken the original in recent years. And for this Andrea's version, we've come up with a tangy and satisfying sauce.

½ cup white wine
½ cup water
1 tablespoon minced carrot
1 tablespoon minced celery
1 teaspoon minced garlic
2 tablespoons vodka
1 tablespoon lemon juice
2 tablespoons minced white onion
1 tablespoon finely chopped Italian parsley
1 tablespoon white vinegar
1 teaspoon salt
8-10 turns freshly ground black pepper
¼ teaspoon crushed red pepper
8 slices thinly sliced fresh high-quality tuna

Combine all the marinade ingredients in a bowl and pour over the slices of fresh tuna. Cover and let marinate in the refrigerator for 1 hour.

Sauce:

¼ cup white wine
1 teaspoon dry mustard
1 tablespoon balsamic vinegar
1 tablespoon Dijon mustard
1 cup extra virgin olive oil
¼ teaspoon salt
¼ teaspoon freshly ground black pepper
1 teaspoon Worcestershire sauce
1 tablespoon finely chopped fresh dill
½ teaspoon Tabasco pepper sauce

Combine the white wine with the dry mustard, and then with the balsamic vinegar and Dijon. Gradually whisk in the olive oil as though making mayonnaise. When emulsified, finish the sauce with all remaining ingredients.

Lemon wedges for garnish

Serve 2 slices of tuna per person atop baby greens, with the sauce spooned over the top. Garnish with lemon wedges. Serves 4.

Clams Casino

The name seems to point us toward Las Vegas in the golden days of Frank Sinatra's Rat Pack, but it's actually a fairly traditional Italian dish long known as "gratinata." It's my favorite way to prepare clams, stuffing the shells and baking them until they're golden brown. So, yes, you can absolutely say these are clams cooked "My Way."

24 littleneck clams
1 cup water

Put the clams in a pan with the water, cover and steam until shells open, discarding any that do not.

2 tablespoons pure olive oil
2 tablespoons chopped white onion
1 tablespoon minced garlic
1 tablespoon chopped oregano
1 tablespoon chopped celery
1 tablespoon chopped red bell pepper
½ teaspoon salt
½ teaspoon crushed red pepper
½ cup unseasoned breadcrumbs
¼ cup grated Pecorino Romano cheese

In a separate pan, heat the pure olive oil and sauté the onion and garlic until caramelized. Stir in the oregano, celery and bell pepper, plus a little of the steaming liquid from the clams. Season with salt and crushed red pepper. Bring to a boil and reduce until syrupy. Remove from the heat and add the breadcrumbs and cheese.

6 slices pancetta, roughly cut into 1-inch squares
Parmesan cheese
Extra virgin olive oil
Celery leaves for garnish

Open the cooled clams and set side by side on a baking sheet. Place a square of pancetta atop each clam and form the stuffing around the two. Use the stuffing to fill the empty top shells as well. Sprinkle with Parmesan and drizzle with extra-virgin olive oil. Set the baking sheet in a preheated 425° oven until the topping turns golden brown, 8-10 minutes. Divide over appetizer plates. Garnish with celery leaves. Serves 4.

Oysters en Brochette Royale

The tradition of cooking on skewers goes far back before the founding of New Orleans, but it's one that certainly has taken hold here. This dish known around town as Oysters en Brochette is a classic served by many restaurants. Still, if you compare our recipe with some of the others in New Orleans, you'll spot quite a few extra touches all aimed at maximizing taste and texture—both wonderful things to maximize, if you ask me.

Sauce:

1/3 cup lemon juice
1/2 cup white wine
1/4 teaspoon hot pepper sauce
1 teaspoon Worcestershire sauce
1/2 teaspoon salt
1 tablespoon all-purpose flour dissolved in 1 tablespoon water

Prepare the sauce by bringing the lemon juice and wine to a boil. Add the pepper and Worcestershire sauces. Season with salt. Over low heat, thicken with the flour dissolved in water.

2 cups heavy cream

In a separate pot, heat the cream to reduce, then simmer. Add the reduced cream to the sauce. Keep warm.

24 slices pancetta or smoked bacon
24 freshly shucked oysters
1/4 cup white wine
1 tablespoon freshly squeezed lemon juice
1 cup water

Crisp the pancetta or bacon in a preheated 400° oven for about 5 minutes. Poach the oysters briefly in the wine and lemon juice. Remove the oysters to a platter and then briefly poach the slices of leek, 4-5 minutes, to make them more pliable. Drain.

1 fresh leek, washed, white parts only

To form the brochettes, lay 2 slices of leek on each slice of pancetta. Set 1 oyster (2 if they're small) on each near the end and roll up with the oyster in the center. Skewer 6 rolled-up oysters on each bamboo skewer and bake in a preheated 425° oven until golden brown and crunchy, 12-14 minutes, turning frequently.

Lemon wedges for garnish

Set 1 skewer on each large appetizer plate and remove the skewer. Spoon the sauce over the top. Garnish with lemon wedges. Serves 4.

Baked Oysters Radosta

Named after a very good customer, this dish is totally in the spirit of New Orleans' love affair with baked oyster casseroles. Of course, it's also in the spirit of what we Italians have been doing with oysters, clams and mussels for probably a thousand years.

½ cup pure olive oil
½ cup chopped white onion
¼ cup minced garlic
1 tablespoon chopped celery
1 tablespoon chopped green onion
3 cups freshly shucked oysters, water reserved
½ cup white wine
1 teaspoon salt
½ teaspoon crushed red pepper
1 teaspoon Worcestershire sauce
1 cup unseasoned breadcrumbs
½ cup grated Romano cheese

Extra-virgin olive oil
Grated Parmesan cheese
Fresh Italian parsley for garnish

Heat the pure olive oil in a large pan and sauté the onion and garlic until caramelized. Then stir in the celery and green onion, sautéing until tender. Add the shucked oysters and wine, bringing mixture to a boil. Season with salt, crushed red pepper and Worcestershire sauce. Remove from heat and stir in the breadcrumbs and Romano, along with enough oyster water to keep the dressing moist.

Lightly coat a baking dish with extra-virgin olive oil, then fill with the oyster mixture and smooth the top with a spoon. Drizzle with olive oil and sprinkle with Parmesan cheese. Bake in a preheated 450° oven until golden brown, 12-14 minutes. Let rest for 5 minutes, then spoon onto appetizer plates. (You can also bake this dressing in individual ramekins.) Garnish with fresh Italian parsley. Serves 4.

Vitello Tonnato

Here is one of my signature dishes in New Orleans, an Italian classic I introduced when I first came to the city as executive chef at the Royal Orleans Hotel. Since many of my first customers at Andrea's were people who knew me from there, I had no choice but to carry this cold Tuscan specialty with me. To this day, I'm delighted to serve it to my guests.

1 (1¼-1½ pound) veal round
1 teaspoon salt
⅛ teaspoon white pepper
3 tablespoons vegetable oil
¼ carrot, sliced into rings
¼ white onion, sliced
1 rib celery, chopped
2 cloves garlic, crushed
1 cup white wine
1 bay leaf
½ teaspoon chopped fresh rosemary
1 cup water

Season the veal with salt and white pepper. Heat the oil in the skillet and brown the veal on all sides. Set the pan into a preheated 450° oven, turning after 5 minutes. After 10 minutes, add the carrot, onion and celery, cooking another 10 minutes. Add the wine, bay leaf, rosemary and water, then return veal to the oven until cooked through, about 45 minutes. Remove the veal and discard other ingredients. Let cool.

Sauce:

¼ pound fresh tuna, poached (or 1 cup canned, rinsed and drained)
8 anchovies
2 tablespoons capers
1½ teaspoon minced garlic
1 tablespoon minced white onion
1 cup freshly prepared mayonnaise
1½ teaspoons freshly squeezed lemon juice
5 drops Tabasco pepper sauce
¼ teaspoon Worcestershire sauce

Prepare the sauce by blending all ingredients in a food processor until anchovies and capers are small but not completely puréed. Thinly slice the cooled veal and divide over 8-10 appetizer plates. Spoon the sauce over the top of the veal. Garnish with strips of anchovy, capers, rosemary sprigs, lemon wedges and a slice of tomato. Serves 8-10.

Eggplant Olympics

Not really a tribute to the original Olympic games, this dish is actually named after a culinary Olympics in New Orleans shortly after I arrived in the late 1970s. I'm proud to say this recipe won the gold medal, and it remains one of my customers' favorites to this day. In New Orleans, as in Italy and Greece, we love stuffing anything that isn't quick enough to get away.

Sauce:

2 tablespoons all-purpose flour
2 cups fish stock
⅓ cup chopped red bell pepper
2 tablespoons Herbsaint liqueur
1 cup heavy cream
½ teaspoon hot pepper sauce
1 tablespoon Worcestershire sauce
1 teaspoon salt
1 cup crawfish tails
1 tablespoon chopped Italian parsley
1 tablespoon chopped green onion

Prepare the sauce by browning the flour without liquid in the oven until dark brown but not burned. Add all remaining ingredients and bring to a boil, simmering to reduce until lush. Keep warm.

1 eggplant, sliced crosswise into 6 rounds
⅓ cup pure olive oil
2 tablespoons chopped white onion
2 tablespoons minced garlic
⅓ cup white wine
12 jumbo shrimp, peeled and deveined
1 tablespoon chopped celery
1 tablespoon chopped green bell pepper
1 tablespoon chopped fresh oregano
1 tablespoon chopped fresh basil
1 tablespoon chopped green onion
1 teaspoon paprika
½ teaspoon chopped fresh thyme leaves
½ teaspoon crushed red pepper
1 tablespoon Herbsaint liqueur
2 cups jumbo lump crabmeat

Hollow into the center of each eggplant round, stopping before cutting through, to form a well. Heat the olive oil in a large pan and sauté the onion and garlic until caramelized, then pour in the white wine. Chop the shrimp along with the eggplant flesh, adding to the pan with the celery, bell pepper, oregano, basil, green onion, paprika, thyme, crushed red pepper and Herbsaint. Gently fold in the crabmeat, cooking over low heat for 5 minutes.

Salt and pepper
All-purpose flour
4 eggs, lightly beaten
Whole milk
Unseasoned breadcrumbs
Vegetable oil

To complete the dish, season the eggplant rounds with salt and pepper, then in sequence dip them in flour, then in the beaten eggs mixed with a little milk and finally in the breadcrumbs. Fry the rounds until golden brown in batches in vegetable oil preheated to 350°, 8-10 minutes per batch. Turn in the oil occasionally. Drain on paper towels.

(continued on next page)

Extra-virgin olive oil
Parmesan cheese
Fresh basil or oregano leaves for garnish

Transfer the drained rounds to a baking pan and top each by forming a mound of the seafood mixture. Drizzle with extra-virgin olive oil and sprinkle with Parmesan cheese. Bake in a preheated 425° oven until golden brown, 8-10 minutes. Serve each topped eggplant on an appetizer plate, with sauce spooned generously over the top. Garnish with basil or oregano leaves. Serves 6.

Mussels Posillipo

Here's a mussel dish that regularly makes believers out of people who don't think they like mussels. It hails from an area around the Bay of Naples, the water I saw every day growing up on my beautiful island of Capri. And if you love this recipe and want to enjoy it often, you can even change things up once in a while by leaving out the tomato and adding a touch of butter at the end.

½ cup pure olive oil
36 fresh mussels, debearded
1 cup white wine
1 cup water

Heat the pure olive oil in a pan. Add the mussels along with the 1 cup of wine and the water, covering to steam for 2-3 minutes. Discard any mussels whose shells don't open during steaming. Remove from the liquid.

⅓ cup extra-virgin olive oil
1 tablespoon minced garlic
½ cup white wine
1 cup fish stock
1 teaspoon crushed red pepper
16 cherry tomatoes
1 tablespoon chopped Italian parsley
1 tablespoon chopped fresh oregano
¼ teaspoon salt
Italian parsley for garnish

In a separate pan, heat the extra-virgin olive oil and caramelize the garlic. Add the ½ cup wine, stock and crushed red pepper. Squeeze the tomatoes through your fingers into the sauce, then add the Italian parsley, oregano and salt. Add the mussels, tossing to coat in the sauce. Bring to a boil then divide into bowls. Garnish with Italian parsley. Serves 4.

Seafood-Stuffed Mirlitons Piccata

Known as mirlitons in New Orleans, with a nod to the city's French heritage, these members of the squash family are called chayote or vegetable pear in the outside world. Whatever you call them, it's hard to beat what happens when you stuff them with wonderful fresh seafood and ladle a bit of lemon-butter piccata sauce over the top.

4 mirlitons
Salt

Poach the mirlitons in salted water for 10 minutes to soften. Cut them in half lengthwise and scoop out the inside. Chop up the tender flesh, leaving the skin to serve as shells for the stuffing.

1/3 cup pure olive oil
1 cup chopped white onion
1/4 cup chopped celery
1/4 cup chopped red bell pepper
1/4 cup chopped green bell pepper
1 tablespoon minced garlic
2 cups chopped fresh fish (snapper, trout, amberjack)
1 cup lump crabmeat
1 tablespoon chopped Italian parsley
1 tablespoon chopped fresh oregano
1 teaspoon salt
1/2 teaspoon crushed red pepper
1/2 cup white wine
1 cup chopped fresh shrimp
1 cup fish stock
1 tablespoon Worcestershire sauce
1/3 cup grated Parmesan cheese
1/2 cup unseasoned breadcrumbs

Heat the olive oil and sauté the onion, celery, bell peppers and garlic until caramelized. Gently incorporate the fish and crabmeat, along with the Italian parsley, oregano, salt and crushed red pepper. Stir in the red wine over medium heat, then add the shrimp and cook 1-2 minutes, just until pink. Add the chopped mirliton. Add the stock, Worcestershire sauce, Parmesan cheese and breadcrumbs, stirring to form a thick, moist stuffing.

Extra-virgin olive oil
Parmesan cheese

Drizzle a baking pan with olive oil and set out the mirliton shells. Mound the stuffing into each shell and sprinkle with Parmesan cheese. Bake in a preheated 400° oven until golden brown, 10-12 minutes.

Sauce:
1/2 cup white wine
1/4 cup lemon juice
1 teaspoon hot pepper sauce
1 tablespoon Worcestershire sauce
1 teaspoon salt
1 1/2 cups softened butter
Basil leaves for garnish

Combine the wine, lemon juice, pepper sauce, Worcestershire sauce and salt in a pan and bring just to a boil. Remove from heat. Stir in the butter a little at a time, whisking to fully incorporate. Transfer the stuffed mirlitons to large appetizer plates and spoon generously with piccata sauce. Garnish with fresh basil leaves. Serves 8.

Stuffed Bell Peppers Anna

If you think you make some good stuffed bell peppers—and most cooks along the Gulf Coast figure they do—don't start writing your awards speech until you sample these.

⅓ cup pure olive oil
2 tablespoons finely chopped white onion
1 tablespoon minced garlic
¼ pound ground beef
¼ pound ground veal
½ pound crumbled Italian sausage
1 tablespoon chopped fresh basil
1 tablespoon chopped green onion
1 tablespoon chopped fresh Italian parsley
1 tablespoon chopped fresh oregano
½ teaspoon crushed red pepper
1 tablespoon chopped red bell pepper
1 tablespoon chopped green bell pepper
1 tablespoon chopped leek, green and white parts
1 tablespoon chopped celery
½ cup white wine
1 teaspoon salt
1 cup unseasoned breadcrumbs
⅓ cup grated Parmesan cheese
1 egg, lightly beaten

4 whole bell peppers (red, green or yellow)
Grated Parmesan cheese
Extra-virgin olive oil
Fresh basil leaves for garnish

Roasted Garlic-Tomato Sauce
7 whole cloves garlic, peeled
2 tablespoons pure olive oil
2 cups crushed tomatoes
2 tablespoons chopped fresh basil
1 teaspoon salt
¼ cup heavy cream

Heat the oil in a sauté pan and sauté the onion and garlic until caramelized. Add the meat and stir until it is cooked through and all the water has evaporated. Add the basil, green onion, parsley, oregano, crushed red pepper, bell peppers, leek and celery. Sauté 3-4 minutes, then pour in the white wine and cook until it evaporates. Season with salt. Remove from the heat and stir in the breadcrumbs, Parmesan cheese and egg.

Stuff the hollowed-out bell peppers. Sprinkle the tops with cheese and drizzle with extra-virgin olive oil. Set the peppers into a baking pan with a little water in the bottom and bake in a preheated 425° oven until tender, 10-12 minutes.

Roast the whole garlic cloves in the olive oil over a hot fire until brown and caramelized. Add the tomatoes, basil, salt and cream, letting the sauce simmer for about 10 minutes so flavors can combine. Purée the sauce until smooth.

To serve, ladle a pool of sauce onto the bottom of 6 appetizer plates. Slice the bell peppers across and set atop each pool of sauce. Garnish with fresh basil leaves. Serves 6.

Crawfish Beignets Rosa

While I love those beignets with powdered sugar in the French Quarter as much as the next person, it's about time we chefs realized the close kinship between New Orleans' legendary fried doughnut and the fritters made with seafood in many corners of the globe. Certainly conch fritters in the Caribbean island come to mind every time I make these treats with Louisiana crawfish.

½ cup whole milk
1 cup all-purpose flour
4 egg yolks, lightly beaten
4 egg whites
½ cup chopped crawfish tails
¼ cup diced red and green bell peppers
½ cup beer
1 teaspoon paprika
1 teaspoon finely chopped fresh Italian parsley
⅛ teaspoon salt
Peanut or vegetable oil for deep frying

In a mixing bowl, combine the milk with the flour, then stir in the egg yolks. Beat the egg whites until stiff, then fold them into the milk mixture. Add all remaining ingredients, stirring until well incorporated. Deep fry in oil preheated to 375°. Remove with a slotted spoon and drain on paper towels. Serve hot. Serves 6.

Calamari Sciue Sciue

For folks out there who are always complaining they don't have time to cook a nice dinner, this dish, which translates as Calamari Quick Quick, should really hit the spot. It is a reminder (and we always seem to need one) that when you put your hands on the best and freshest ingredients, the best idea is sometimes to let them stand on their own.

½ cup pure olive oil
1 tablespoon minced garlic
½ cup crushed red pepper
2 cups cleaned and chopped calamari
16 cherry tomatoes
½ cup white wine
1 tablespoon chopped fresh oregano
1 tablespoon chopped Italian parsley
1 teaspoon salt
Toasted rustic bread slices

Heat the olive oil in a pan and sauté the garlic until caramelized. Stir in the crushed red pepper, then add the calamari and sauté until golden brown. Squeeze the cherry tomatoes through your fingers into the pan. Add the wine, followed by the oregano and Italian parsley. Season with salt. Bring the mixture to a boil and serve with toasted rustic bread. Serves 4.

Four-Cheese Soufflé Sandra   Somehow, people have come to think of making soufflés as difficult—like, "Don't walk on that street, there's a soufflé in the oven somewhere and it might fall!" In some ways, making a soufflé is as easy as breathing—that's what the word means in French, after all, a reference to the way the hot air inside makes the soufflé rise. Whatever bravery you think this recipe requires, I promise it will be worth it.

½ quart whole milk
½ teaspoon ground nutmeg

In a saucepan, bring the milk and nutmeg just to a boil.

½ cup all-purpose flour
8 egg yolks, lightly beaten
4 ounces Asiago cheese, finely chopped
2 ounces goat cheese, finely chopped
2 ounces Fontina cheese, finely chopped
½ cup grated Parmesan cheese

In a separate pot, melt the butter and mix in the flour to form a roux. When mixed, add in the milk mixture and simmer for 5 minutes. Let cool for 10 minutes, then add the egg yolks and four cheeses.

8 egg whites
½ teaspoon paprika
¼ teaspoon baking powder

Whip the egg whites until foamy and combine with the batter, along with the paprika and baking powder. Pour into 8 buttered and floured individual ramekins and set these in a pan with 2 inches of water. Bake in a preheated 425° oven for 20-30 minutes, until the soufflés have risen and turned golden. Serve with additional Parmesan cheese. Serves 8.

Lumache al Italiano

I guess we have French restaurants to thank for making snails or escargots a bit more familiar in this country. Still if the only snails you've ever tasted have taken the form and flavor of French escargots, then we Italians are here to tell you: You are in for a treat.

¼ cup pure olive oil
½ cup chopped shallots
1 tablespoon minced garlic
32 snails, out of shells
½ cup white wine
¼ teaspoon crushed red pepper
1 cup chopped Roma tomatoes
1 tablespoon chopped fresh basil
1 tablespoon chopped fresh oregano
1 tablespoon chopped fresh Italian parsley
1 tablespoon Worcestershire sauce
¼ cup unsalted butter
½ teaspoon salt
½ teaspoon freshly ground black pepper
2 sage leaves, finely chopped

Heat the olive oil in a large skillet and sauté the onion and garlic until caramelized, then add the snails and stir for 2-3 minutes. Add the white wine and cook until evaporated, then add the crushed red pepper, tomato, basil, oregano, parsley and Worcestershire sauce. Simmer for 5 minutes, then enrich the sauce with the butter. Season with salt, pepper and sage. Divide the snails into ramekins or small bowls, along with slices of grilled rustic bread. Serves 4.

Crabmeat au Gratin Domenico

The French get a lot of the credit for making crabmeat au gratin a household word in the United States, but I'll bet that's just because the Italian word *gratinatta* has too many syllables. The concept is every bit as Italian as it is French. And truth be told, some of guests say this is the best crabmeat au gratin they've ever tasted.

⅓ cup unsalted butter
2 tablespoons chopped white onion
1 teaspoon minced garlic
2 cups chopped mushrooms
⅓ cup chopped green onions
1 pound jumbo lump crabmeat
¼ teaspoon Tabasco pepper sauce

Melt the butter in a skillet and sauté the onion and garlic until caramelized, then stir in the mushrooms and green onion. After 2-3 minutes, combine off the heat with the crabmeat and Tabasco.

2 tablespoons unsalted butter
2 tablespoons all-purpose flour
2 cups whole milk
2 cups shredded Swiss cheese
½ cup heavy cream
2 tablespoons Parmesan cheese
1 teaspoon salt

In a separate pan, melt the butter and combine with the flour to make a smooth white roux. Fully incorporate the milk, then remove from the heat and add the Swiss cheese and the crab mixture. Stir in the cream, Parmesan cheese and salt.

2 tablespoons Parmesan cheese
2 tablespoons unseasoned breadcrumbs
Additional butter

Butter 4 ramekins and spoon in the crabmeat mixture. Make a topping by combining the Parmesan with the breadcrumbs. Sprinkle this over the top along with 1 pat of butter each. Set the ramekins on a baking pan and bake in a preheated 400° oven until the top is golden brown, 8-10 minutes. Let the ramekins sit for 3-4 minutes before serving. Serves 4.

Crespelle di Formaggio Sorrento

Since so many Italian cheeses have different flavors and different ways of reacting to heat, it makes sense to us Italians sometimes to combine as many different ones as we can get our hands on. You might say we want to have our cheese and eat it too! These incredible appetizer crepes use no fewer than seven beloved cheeses. Feel free to experiment with more or different ones, as we always will. But for now, our favorites are in this recipe.

6 ounces Fontina cheese
6 ounces Swiss cheese
6 ounces fresh mozzarella
6 ounces Belle Paese
1 cup grated Parmesan cheese
1 cup ricotta cheese
1 tablespoon minced garlic
2 tablespoons finely chopped onion
1 tablespoon chopped fresh basil
1 tablespoon chopped fresh parsley
1 teaspoon ground nutmeg
1 egg yolk
1 cup dairy sour cream
½ cup cream cheese
1 cup finely chopped ham
1 cup unseasoned breadcrumbs

In a double boiler over hot water, melt the first 6 cheeses and stir until they are incorporated, then let cool. Mix in the garlic, onion, basil, parsley, nutmeg, egg yolk, sour cream and cream cheese, stirring with a rubber spatula. Incorporate the ham and breadcrumbs.

24 prepared crêpes
Unsalted butter
1 cup water

Fill each crêpe with about ¼ cup of the filling, rolling each up and pressing together to seal the ends. Butter a pan or baking dish. Arrange the crêpes on the butter and pour on the water. Cover with aluminum foil and set the pan in a preheated 375° oven until heated through, 10-12 minutes.

Sauce:
¼ cup pure olive oil
1 tablespoon chopped fresh sage leaves
½ cup chopped ham
2 tablespoons white wine
1 cup unsalted butter
2 tablespoons grated Parmesan cheese

Meanwhile, prepare the sauce by heating the olive oil in a skillet and stir-frying the sage with the ham. Deglaze with the wine and stir in the butter, cooking until lightly browned. Remove from the heat and stir in the Parmesan. Spoon over the crêpes. Serves 8-10.

Seafood-Stuffed Eggplant

It's totally fine that everybody loves crab-cakes these days—at least until you taste what happens when the delights of this classic collide with the delights of New Orleans-style panéed eggplant. As any New Orleans Italian will tell you, seafood and eggplant are a marriage made in heaven—or, even better, in Barataria Bay!

2 medium eggplants, cut lengthwise
6 ounces water

Preheat the oven to 400°. Wash the eggplant halves. With a pointed knife cut shallow lengthwise lines in each piece. Turn upside down and put in a baking pan with 6 ounces of water and bake for 20 minutes. Let the halves cool and then scoop out the flesh. Set aside the skins for stuffing.

½ cup pure olive oil
1 tablespoon minced onions
1 teaspoon minced garlic
1 cup chopped celery
½ cup chopped leek

Sauté the onions, garlic, celery and leek in the olive oil until caramelized.

4 sea scallops, chopped
½ cup crawfish tails
1 cup peeled and deveined shrimp
½ cup mild fish, cut in chunks
½ cup jumbo lump crabmeat
½ cup white wine
1 teaspoon salt
½ teaspoon crushed red pepper
1 tablespoon chopped oregano
1 tablespoon chopped basil
2 tablespoons grated Parmesan cheese
½ cup breadcrumbs, if needed to thicken

Add the scallops, crawfish, shrimp, fish and crabmeat. Add the wine and bring to a boil. Chop the cooled eggplant and add it to the pot. Add salt, pepper, oregano and basil. Bring everything to a boil. Remove from heat. Add 2 tablespoons of Parmesan cheese. Mix very well. The stuffing should be firm. If it is not thick enough, add ½ cup of breadcrumbs.

Additional grated Parmesan cheese

Fill the eggplant skins and sprinkle parmesan cheese on top. Return to the baking pan with water and bake at 400° for 8-10 minutes. Serve with linguine and tomato sauce Serves 4.

Andrea's Pizza Party Murray

When we had the idea of creating the best pizza ever for this cookbook, the closest we could get was the *four* best pizzas ever. What a miserable day around the kitchen *that* was, with just about every employee finding himself or herself near enough to grab a slice. All in the name of scholarly research, of course! And the idea of Andrea's Pizza Party was born.

Pizza Crust:

2 pounds bread flour, preferably Farina "00"
1 tablespoon dry yeast dissolved in
2 tablespoons lukewarm water
3 cups lukewarm water
1 teaspoon salt
2 teaspoons pure olive oil
Additional flour
Semolina flour

To make 8 individual pizza crusts, measure the flour into a large mixer with a bread hook set on low speed and combine with the yeast dissolved in water. Stop and let sit for 2-3 minutes. Again on low speed, pour in 2 cups of the water with the salt and olive oil. Gradually add in the remaining water, until the dough starts to pull away from the side of the bowl and form an elastic ball. Run the mixer on high speed for 3-4 minutes, until the ball becomes tight.

Spread additional flour on a flat, dry surface and tear the ball into eight approximately equal portions (weighing about 6 ounces each). Roll each smaller ball in the flour until smooth and dry. Set on a floured baking sheet, cover with a towel and let rise in a warm place for 30 minutes. Once the dough has risen, work each ball out into a circle on a floured surface, using your hands or a rolling pin. Coat a baking sheet with semolina and set out pizza crusts. Partially bake in a preheated 400° oven. Set aside to cool.

Pizza Bianca:

2 tablespoons pure olive oil
1 cup thinly sliced white onion
1 tablespoon minced garlic
1 tablespoon extra-virgin olive oil
1 (4-ounce) package goat cheese
1 cup crumbled gorgonzola
1 cup shredded mozzarella
4 ounces Bel Paese cheese
1 tablespoon chopped fresh oregano
¼ cup chopped fresh basil
¼ teaspoon crushed red pepper
2 tablespoons grated Parmesan cheese
Extra-virgin olive oil

Make 2 Pizzas Bianca by heating the olive oil and stirring the onion and garlic until caramelized. Spread over 2 crusts and drizzle with olive oil. Divide the goat cheese, gorgonzola, mozzarella and Bel Paese over the pizza. Sprinkle with oregano, basil, crushed red pepper and Parmesan. Drizzle with additional olive oil. Bake until golden and bubbly, 8-10 minutes.

(Continued on next page)

Pizza Marinara:

2 cups chopped Roma tomatoes
2 tablespoons capers
6-8 anchovy fillets, finely chopped
1 tablespoon chopped fresh oregano
¼ teaspoon crushed red pepper

Make 2 Pizzas Marinara by dividing the chopped tomatoes, capers, anchovies and oregano over the crusts, then sprinkling with crushed red pepper. Cover with mozzarella and olive oil, then with a sprinkling of Parmesan. Bake until golden and bubbly, 8-10 minutes.

Pizza Amalfi:

3 cups chopped Roma tomatoes
¼ cup chopped fresh basil
1 tablespoon minced garlic
1 tablespoon chopped fresh oregano
1 teaspoon salt
1 tablespoon extra-virgin olive oil
¼ teaspoon crushed red pepper
10 ounces fresh mozzarella cheese
Black olives, pitted and crushed
1 tablespoon Parmesan cheese
4 sun-dried tomatoes, thinly sliced

Make 2 Pizzas Amalfi by crushing the tomatoes with your fingers into a bowl, then stirring in the basil, garlic, oregano, salt, olive oil and crushed red pepper. Spread over the 2 crusts, then top with mozzarella and black olives. Sprinkle with Parmesan, sun-dried tomato strips and a little oil from the sun-dried tomatoes. Bake until golden and bubbly, 8-10 minutes.

Pizza Andrea:

3 links cooked Italian sausage, casing removed, chopped
8 cherry tomatoes, sliced
1 tablespoon chopped sun-dried tomato
1 teaspoon chopped fresh oregano
¼ cup chopped fresh basil
½ avocado, thinly sliced
¼ cup extra-virgin olive oil
1 teaspoon minced garlic
½ teaspoon crushed red pepper
1 cup crumbled gorgonzola cheese
2 tablespoons Parmesan cheese

Make 2 Pizzas Andrea by covering 2 crusts with the chopped cooked sausage. Top with sliced cherry tomatoes, sun-dried tomato, oregano, basil and avocado slices. Mix the olive oil with the garlic and drizzle onto pizzas. Sprinkle on the gorgonzola and top with crushed red pepper and Parmesan. Bake until golden and bubbly, 8-10 minutes.

Slice the 8 pizzas into 32 wedges—and let the party begin!

Insalate

Recipe on page 82

Insalate Caprese

Since Capri is my home, I've always enjoyed serving this wonderful (oh so simple!) salad to all my guests. Compared to most of the wacky salads chefs come up with these days, this layering of fresh tomato slices and our homemade buffalo mozzarella is hard to beat, especially in the summertime around New Orleans when local "Creole tomatoes" are at their absolute peak of flavor. For this salad, always use the most flavorful—meaning, least industrial—tomatoes you can get your hands on. Taste this famous salad from Capri and you'll see why!

Dressing:
⅔ cup pure olive oil
1 tablespoon finely chopped white onions
½ teaspoon minced garlic
2 fresh basil leaves, chopped
1 teaspoon chopped fresh oregano
½ teaspoon salt
½ teaspoon freshly ground black pepper

Prepare the dressing by stirring together all ingredients.

1 cup mixed baby greens or Boston Bibb lettuce
1 tablespoon pure olive oil
⅛ teaspoon salt
2 Creole tomatoes, cut in ½-inch slices
¾ pound fresh buffalo mozzarella, in 8 slices

Lightly coat the mixed greens with olive oil and salt, then divide them over 4 salad plates. Top each bed of greens with a slice of tomato, then mozzarella, then tomato, then mozzarella. Drizzle the dressing over the top and around the plate. Serves 4.

Andrea's Salad with Creamy Italian Dressing

As people ask for this salad every day at Andrea's, we get a lot of requests for the recipe as well. As usual, it's not rocket science to make even the dressing—we just have to be careful to follow our own recipe every day. You all will let us know if we don't!

Creamy Italian Dressing:

4 eggs, lightly beaten
1 tablespoon Dijon or other mustard
1 tablespoon English dry mustard
½ cup balsamic vinegar
2 cups pure olive oil
1 cup extra-virgin olive oil
1 cup vegetable oil
¼ cup lemon juice
2 teaspoons salt
1 teaspoon hot pepper sauce
1 tablespoon Worcestershire sauce
2 tablespoons minced garlic
½ teaspoon black pepper
⅓ cup heavy cream

To prepare the dressing in a stand-up mixer, combine the eggs, mustard, dry mustard and vinegar, then slowly incorporate the oils, lemon juice, salt, pepper sauce, Worcestershire, garlic and pepper until emulsified. (Makes 6 cups. Remainder keeps well in the refrigerator about 1 month.)

3 cups mixed baby greens
1 tablespoon grated Parmesan cheese
2 Roma tomatoes, chopped
3 fresh mushrooms, chopped
1 green onion, chopped
¼ avocado, sliced

In a bowl, toss the greens with the cheese and ⅓ cup of dressing. Divide onto salad plates and top with tomato, mushrooms, green onion and avocado. Serves 2.

(pictured on p. 79)

Classic Caesar Salad

When an Italian named Cesare Cardini invented this salad tableside in Tijuana, Mexico, in the early 1900s, little could he know it would become a near-mandatory part of every Italian restaurant's menu ever since. This version is not only close to Cardini's original but it's one our guests at Andrea's come back to enjoy over and over again.

2 egg yolks, lightly beaten
1 tablespoon Dijon mustard
Juice of 1 lemon
8 anchovy fillets, finely chopped
1 tablespoon oil from anchovies
¼ cup grated Parmesan cheese
1 teaspoon salt
2 teaspoon Worcestershire sauce
1 teaspoon hot pepper sauce
1 tablespoon balsamic vinegar
1 cup homemade croutons
4 grinds black pepper from a mill
8 cups chopped Romaine lettuce

In a large bowl, using a fork, gradually combine the egg yolks with the mustard and lemon juice. Add the anchovy fillets and anchovy oil, along with the Parmesan, salt, Worcestershire, pepper sauce, balsamic vinegar and black pepper. Add the croutons and Romaine, tossing in the dressing to coat thoroughly. Divide onto salad plates. Serves 4.

Fresh Fennel and Blood Orange Salad

To me, the flavors of fennel and blood orange are associated with Sicily. The first, Sicilians love to put in dishes when you'd least expect, contributing a mild hint of licorice. The second, for all its dazzling bright red color, is a reflection of the wealth of citrus brought to the Mediterranean island by wave after wave of Arab conquerors.

4 blood oranges
2 bulbs fresh fennel
1 tablespoon orange-infused extra-virgin olive oil
⅓ cup dry white wine
1 tablespoon chopped white onion
1 teaspoon minced garlic
¼ teaspoon crushed red pepper
Salt and black pepper to taste
Mixed baby greens

Zest the oranges and reserve the zest. Peel the oranges and slice them across to form 12 circles. Cut the rest in wedges. Cut open the fennel and remove the hard center. Thinly slice the rest, wash it and drain it. Mix the orange wedges with the sliced fennel, then toss with the orange-infused olive oil, the wine, the onion, the garlic and crushed red pepper. Season to taste with salt and pepper.

Arrange 3 orange circles on each salad plate and top with a few of the mixed greens. Spoon the fennel-blood orange mixture from the bowl. Decorate the plate, if desired, with additional splashes of orange olive oil. Serves 4.

Steamed Asparagus with Honey Mustard Dressing

I'm happy to see that so many people enjoy honey mustard dressing these days—there must be two dozen versions at the supermarket. Ours, of course, is not only more flavorful than some but the perfect accent to the perfect asparagus.

Honey Mustard Dressing:
2 tablespoons Dijon mustard
⅓ cup white vinegar
2 teaspoons freshly squeezed lemon juice
1 cup vegetable oil
1 cup pure olive oil
1 tablespoon balsamic vinegar
½ cup honey
1 tablespoon sugar
1 teaspoon salt

To prepare the dressing in a stand-up mixer, incorporate the mustard, vinegar and lemon juice, then slowly stream in the oils as though making homemade mayonnaise. Mix in the remaining dressing ingredients until fully emulsified. (Makes about 3 cups. Keeps well in the refrigerator for up to 1 month.)

Mixed salad greens
4 slices Creole or beefsteak tomato
16 asparagus spears, steamed but still crisp
¼ cup sliced red onion

Arrange 2 or 3 leaves of salad greens on plates. Top each plate with 2 slices of tomato, 8 asparagus spears and a few slices of onion. Drizzle with about 2 tablespoons of dressing per person. Serves 2.

Artichoke and Baby Green Salad

The dressing incorporates the most ingredients here; but if you love artichoke hearts the way I do, this simple salad is sure to become a new favorite.

Balsamic Herb Vinaigrette:
1 tablespoon Dijon mustard
1 cup balsamic vinegar
1 cup pure olive oil
1 cup extra-virgin olive oil
⅓ cup finely chopped onion
1 tablespoon minced garlic
1 teaspoon salt
1 teaspoon freshly ground black pepper
1 teaspoon hot pepper sauce
1 tablespoon chopped fresh oregano
1 tablespoon chopped fresh basil
1 tablespoon chopped Italian parsley

To prepare the dressing in a stand-up mixer, incorporate the mustard and vinegar, then gradually add the oil as though making homemade mayonnaise. Add the remaining dressing ingredients until smooth and emulsified. (Makes about 3 cups. Remainder keeps well in the refrigerator up to 1 month.)

1 cup fresh artichoke hearts
1½ cups arugula
1 cup mixed baby greens
1 teaspoon Parmesan cheese

In a large bowl, toss the artichoke hearts and both kinds of greens in ½ cup of the dressing. Serve on salad plates, sprinkled with Parmesan cheese. Serves 2.

Baby Romaine with Blue Cheese Dressing

This is a salad I love to spring on unsuspecting friends who think they don't like blue cheese dressing. The dressing has a lot of wonderful flavors, all in perfect balance.

Dressing:
2 eggs
3 additional egg yolks
1 tablespoon Dijon mustard
1½ tablespoon minced garlic
1 cup pure olive oil
¼ cup extra-virgin olive oil
1 cup vegetable oil
1 tablespoon red wine vinegar
1 teaspoon white vinegar
1 tablespoon dairy sour cream
1 teaspoon celery salt
1 teaspoon salt

To prepare the dressing in a stand-up mixer, combine the eggs, yolks, mustard and garlic, then gradually pour in the oils as though making homemade mayonnaise. Add all remaining dressing ingredients except the blue cheese until smooth and emulsified. Gently, using a plastic spatula, blend in the crumbles of cheese. (Makes about 4 cups. Remainder keeps well in the refrigerator up to 1 month.)

(continued on next page)

1 teaspoon freshly ground black pepper
1 teaspoon hot pepper sauce
1 teaspoon freshly squeezed lemon juice
1 teaspoon Worcestershire sauce
1 tablespoon balsamic vinegar
3 cups crumbled blue cheese

3 cups chopped Romaine lettuce

In a large bowl, toss the Romaine with ⅔ cup of dressing. Serve on salad plates. Serves 2.

Spinach Salad Amaro Dolce

Yes, the name does mean "sweet and sour" spinach salad, the result of Italy's long fascination with balancing those two apparent opposites on one plate. Of course, anyone who's lived in Italy will understand that the history of the republic is one long story of balancing sweet and sour. So why not on a spinach salad?

Amaro Dolce Dressing:
1 tablespoon Dijon mustard
1 tablespoon white vinegar
1 tablespoon red wine vinegar
2 whole eggs
4 egg yolks
¼ cup pure olive oil
2 cups vegetable oil
1 tablespoon lemon juice
1 tablespoon Worcestershire
1 teaspoon hot pepper sauce
¾ teaspoon salt
1 tablespoon pineapple juice
1 tablespoon apple juice
1 tablespoon grapefruit juice
1 tablespoon honey
1 tablespoon balsamic vinegar

To prepare the dressing in a stand-up mixer, incorporate the mustard with the vinegars, eggs and additional yolks, blending until smooth. Gradually stream in the oils as though making homemade mayonnaise, followed by all remaining dressing ingredients, whisking until fully emulsified. (Makes 1½ cups. Keeps well in the refrigerator up to 1 month.)

2 cups fresh spinach leaves
1 hard-boiled egg, quartered
1 tablespoon crumbled cooked bacon
1 tablespoon roasted pinenuts
2 mushrooms, sliced

In a bowl, toss the spinach with about ½ cup of dressing and divide onto salad plates. Top with egg quarters, bacon and mushrooms. Serves 2.

Bella Vista Salad

We didn't want to close out our salad section without this amazing bit of business, a little more complicated than your typical salad but a great deal more exciting as well. Surely the cheese-and-herb-stuffed "beggar's purse" would make this count as a special occasion dish all by itself, right along with a name in Italian that means "beautiful sight." Just make sure you have special occasions often.

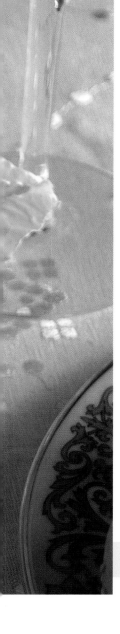

Cheese Stuffing:

2 ounces Fontina cheese
2 ounces fresh mozzarella cheese
2 ounces goat cheese
2 ounces cream cheese
2 tablespoons sour cream
2 ounces Bel Paese cheese
2 ounces ricotta cheese
2 tablespoons grated Parmesan
1 tablespoon chopped Italian parsley
1 tablespoon chopped fresh basil
1 teaspoon minced garlic
1 teaspoon salt
1 teaspoon hot pepper sauce

Mix all ingredients in a food processor or with a hand mixer until smooth.

2 (4-layer) sheets phyllo dough

Lay out the phyllo sheets on a flat surface, cut in half with a sharp knife and then cut in half again. Coat 8 porcelain or enamel baking cups with butter and press a piece of phyllo down into each, creating a well for the stuffing. Divide the stuffing among the cups, then twist together the phyllo sticking up to form a closed phyllo "beggar's purse." Set the cups in the refrigerator while preheating the oven to 400°. Bake until golden brown, 10-12 minutes.

2 Belgian endives, leaves torn off and set in water (24 leaves)
2 cups arugula
2 cups mixed baby greens
8 sliced Portobello mushrooms, lightly grilled, sliced into sticks
8 tablespoons Balsamic Herb Vinaigrette (see recipe p. 86)
16 slices Roma tomato

Meanwhile, arrange 3 slices of endive on each salad plate, fanned out. Top each arugula leaf with 1 stick of grilled mushroom. Toss all the salad greens with the balsamic vinaigrette. Mound the greens atop the mushroom-topped endive leaves. Garnish each plate with 2 slices of tomato. Remove the "purses" from the oven and set each on a plate next to the salad. Serves 8.

Zuppe

Seafood Chowder Bridgette

Few things in all of Italian cooking are more nourishing or more soul-satisfying than a soup like this seafood chowder. For one thing, while it looks like it has a lot of ingredients, like many soups it's delightfully easy to make. And for another thing, if it looks wintry and warming and possibly unfit for our Deep South (or Capri!) summers, nothing could be farther from the truth. The main thing you taste is the wonderful, light fish stock, outfitted only with the freshest seafood and vegetables. This chowder, therefore, is terrific any season of the year.

½ cup pure olive oil
½ cup finely chopped white onion
1 tablespoon minced garlic
1 cup finely chopped carrots
1 cup finely chopped celery
1 cup finely chopped leek
1 head fresh fennel, finely chopped
2 cups chopped canned tomatoes, with juice
4 cups fish stock
2 cups water
2 cups finely chopped potato

Heat the oil in a large soup or stock pot, then sauté the onion with the garlic. Sauté the carrot, celery, leek and fennel until they begin to caramelize, then add the tomatoes with juice, fish stock and water. Bring to a boil, reduce heat and simmer. Add the potatoes and cook until tender, about 20 minutes.

2 teaspoons salt
1 teaspoon crushed red pepper
¼ cup chopped fresh basil
1 tablespoon chopped fresh Italian parsley
1 tablespoon chopped fresh oregano
1 tablespoon Worcestershire sauce
2 cups cut-up white fish fillets
8 large shrimp, cut into bite-sized pieces
1 cup crawfish tails, with fat
Chopped fresh Italian parsley
Toasted rustic bread rounds

Add the salt, red pepper, basil, parsley, oregano and Worcestershire. With 8-10 minutes left, add the fish. When potatoes are tender, add the shrimp and crawfish. Bring to a boil and serve immediately, garnished with Italian parsley. Toasted rustic bread is perfect with this chowder. Serves 8-10.

Stracciatella Frank Francis

It's tempting to presume that only the Chinese really love "eggdrop soup." Well, we're not sure if Marco Polo (as usual) had anything to do with it, but this soup named after a good friend of mine is better than a lot of the eggdrop soup you're likely to find. And it's more colorful too!

1 cup chicken stock
1 cup beef stock

Heat the stocks in a pot until boiling, then reduce heat to a vigorous simmer.

2 eggs, beaten
1 teaspoon chopped fresh oregano
1 tablespoon chopped fresh Italian parsley
1 cup chopped fresh baby spinach leaves
⅓ cup grated Parmesan cheese
¼ teaspoon salt
¼ teaspoon crushed red pepper

In a bowl, combine the eggs with all remaining ingredients. Pour the egg mixture into the simmering stocks and stir until egg is cooked, 1 minute or less. Serve in soup bowls, with additional Parmesan if desired. Serves 4.

Tuscan White Bean Soup

In the beautiful hills and vineyards around Renaissance Florence on the River Arno, winters can actually be cold and long. And considering how many people live in houses built centuries ago, things like insulation and heating are catch-as-catch-can, even for families that have been wealthy for generations. That means that soups like this cannellini classic are indispensable from the cooking of every Tuscan, rich and poor alike. And it's so flavorful, you really don't have to wait until the insulation and heat go out at your house!

2 links Italian sausage, casing removed, cut up
½ cup pure olive oil
1 cup finely chopped carrots
1 cup finely chopped celery, with leaves
1 cup finely chopped white onion
1 tablespoon minced garlic
½ teaspoon crushed red pepper
2 cups chopped canned tomatoes, with juice
4 cups beef stock
2 cups chicken stock
4 cups cooked cannellini (Italian white kidney) beans

In a soup kettle or stock pot, brown the sausage in the olive oil, breaking up any large pieces to render fat and cook the meat through. Add the carrot, celery, white onion, garlic and red pepper, stirring to caramelize. Add the tomatoes and the two stocks. When the broth is bubbling hot, add the beans. Lower the heat to a simmer, cover and cook for about 1 hour, until the beans have begun to break up and thicken the soup.

⅓ cup chopped fresh basil
1 tablespoon chopped fresh oregano
1 teaspoon salt
¼ teaspoon freshly ground black pepper
2 cups uncooked small pasta
Grated Parmesan cheese

Add the basil and oregano. Season with salt and pepper. Add the pasta and cook just until al dente, 5-6 minutes. Serve in bowls sprinkled with Parmesan cheese. Serves 8-10.

Oysters Rockefeller Soup

Considering the popularity of the baked appetizer Oysters Rockefeller in old-line New Orleans restaurants, it was only a matter of time before we chefs started working to extend the flavor combination to other parts of your meal. This soup is certainly one of our greatest success stories, bridging the gap between the textbook Oysters Rockefeller and traditional Creole Oysters Stewed in Cream.

½ cup unsalted butter
⅓ cup pure olive oil
2 tablespoons chopped white onion
1 tablespoon minced garlic
1 cup all-purpose flour
4 cups fish stock
2 cups oyster "water" from oysters

2 cups heavy cream
½ cup chopped celery
½ cup chopped leek, green and white parts
¾ tablespoons Herbsaint liqueur
2 cups raw oysters (about 30)
3 teaspoons salt
2 tablespoons Worcestershire sauce
1 teaspoon hot pepper sauce
2 cups chopped spinach

Heat the butter with the olive oil in a soup kettle or stock pot. Sauté the onion and garlic, stirring to caramelize them. Add the flour and stir to make a white roux, just letting it cook but not start to brown. Gradually add the fish stock, whisking until it's incorporated and smooth. No lumps! Add the oyster water and bring to a boil.

Meanwhile, in a separate pan, bring the cream to a boil—but don't let it burn—and add it to the soup. Add the celery and leek, heating until thickened. Pour in the Herbsaint and oysters. Season with salt, Worcestershire and hot pepper sauce. Add the spinach and bring to a boil. Serves 8.

Italian Wedding Soup

Sometimes you see versions of this soup featuring actual meatballs, especially at Italian-American gatherings with roots in Sicily. May I suggest a slightly different route to a wonderful soup—and, we hope, a happy life for the bride and groom. And considering the number of couples we've cooked for over the years and the number of their children we're cooking for now, there must be something nourishing in this recipe.

4 cups beef stock
2 cups chicken stock
4 eggs, beaten
1 cup unseasoned breadcrumbs
½ cup grated Parmesan cheese
¼ cup chopped fresh oregano
¼ cup chopped fresh Italian parsley
Salt and pepper to taste
2 cups chopped fresh spinach
2 teaspoons salt
½ teaspoon crushed red pepper
1 tablespoon chopped fresh basil
Additional grated Parmesan cheese

Heat the two kinds of stock in a soup kettle or stock pot. In a bowl, combine the eggs with the breadcrumbs, cheese, oregano and parsley, seasoning with salt and pepper. Once a dough is formed, roll pieces into small balls about the size of the tip of your thumb (makes about 32). Carefully drop these dumplings into the hot broth, a few at a time so the broth stays hot. Add the spinach, then season with salt and crushed red pepper. Stir in the basil. Bring to a boil. Stir in additional Parmesan cheese, about ½ cup. Serves 8.

Turtle Soup Henry

In an Old World touch of its own, New Orleans continues to adore and consume oceans of turtle soup. When green sea turtles were placed on the endangered list, New Orleanians prepared this recipe with any substitution they could think of, from alligator on down. Or up, depending on your point of view. Now that turtles are back in full force, we can all make turtle soup the old-fashioned way—with turtle!

1¾ pounds boneless turtle meat
1 gallon fresh water

Boil the turtle meat in 1 gallon of water until it starts to get tender, about 30 minutes, skimming the impurities off the surface. Drain and chop the meat, reserving the turtle stock you have made.

½ cup extra-virgin olive oil
1 cup chopped white onion
1 cup chopped carrot
1 cup chopped celery
1 tablespoon minced garlic
¼ cup tomato paste
½ cup all-purpose flour
1 cup white wine
1 gallon fresh water
1 tablespoon chopped fresh Italian parsley
1 tablespoon chopped fresh sage leaves
½ tablespoon chopped fresh thyme
2 bay leaves

Heat the olive oil in a large pot and sauté the onion, carrot, celery and garlic until they are caramelized, then stir in the tomato paste and ½ cup of flour, cooking for 2-3 minutes. Add the wine and whisk to get a smooth paste, then add the remaining water and bring to a boil. Add the parsley, sage, thyme and bay leaves.

1 teaspoon salt
1 teaspoon white pepper
Pulp of 1 lemon
8 whole cloves
⅓ cup all-purpose flour
¼ cup vegetable oil
1 tablespoon Worcestershire sauce
½ teaspoon Tabasco pepper sauce
2 hard-boiled eggs, chopped
Dry sherry

Pour in the turtle stock. Season with salt and pepper. Return to a boil for 1½ hours. Purée the soup in a food processor. Add the lemon pulp and cloves. Add the turtle meat and reduce heat to a simmer. Make a medium-dark roux by stirring the flour with the vegetable oil in a separate pan, then whisk it into the soup. Season with the Worcestershire and Tabasco. Serve in bowls with chopped eggs and a splash of sherry. Serves 12-14.

Tomato Bisque Patrizia

At the height of summer, in many parts of Italy as in many parts of the United States, it's time for tomatoes. Since the flavor of commercial tomatoes these days can leave a lot to be desired, any time you get your hands on tomatoes you've grown yourself or tomatoes purchased from a small-time farmer, you should do anything and everything you can think of in the kitchen to celebrate. Actually, this bright red bisque can be made well enough with any tomato, but the better the tomato, the better your bisque.

½ cup pure olive oil
½ cup finely chopped white onion
1 tablespoon minced garlic
½ cup finely chopped leek
½ cup finely chopped carrot
½ cup finely chopped celery
1½ lbs. fresh Roma or other tomatoes, coarsely chopped
⅓ cup tomato paste
½ cup dry red wine
2 bay leaves
1 teaspoon crushed red pepper
15 cups chicken or beef stock

Heat the olive oil in a soup kettle or stock pot and sauté the onion and garlic until caramelized. Add the leek, carrot and celery, stirring until they are golden brown. Add the tomatoes and tomato paste, followed by the wine, bay leaves, red pepper and stock. Bring to a boil and simmer until the flavors meld, about 45 minutes.

6 fresh basil leaves
1 cup uncooked white rice
1 teaspoon salt
2 cups heavy cream
2 tablespoons Worcestershire sauce
¼ cup chopped fresh basil

Add the basil leaves, rice and salt, cooking until the rice is tender, about 30 minutes. Remove from the heat. Purée until smooth and return to the pot. Add the cream, chopped basil and Worcestershire, along with salt to taste. Simmer until the bisque coats the back of a spoon. Serves 12-14.

My home-grown tomatoes

Minestrone Pietro

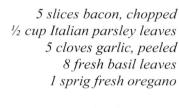

In Italian, *minestra* is a satisfying soup—which means that minestrone is a bigger, even more satisfying one. A giant soup, if you will. A super soup. And that's the role that minestrone has come to play all over the world—a terrific, full-meal of a soup packed with everything the human body needs for nourishment.

5 slices bacon, chopped
½ cup Italian parsley leaves
5 cloves garlic, peeled
8 fresh basil leaves
1 sprig fresh oregano

Prepare the "pastetta" in a food processor by pulsing together the bacon, parsley, garlic, basil and oregano.

1 cup red kidney beans
¼ pound smoked pork
½ cup pure olive oil
1 cup chopped white onion
1 cup chopped carrots
1 cup chopped celery
1 tablespoon minced garlic
1 leek, white part only, chopped
2 tablespoons tomato paste
2 quarts chicken or beef stock (or combination)
2 bay leaves
1 large white potato, peeled and diced
1 large zucchini, coarsely chopped

Soak the red beans in water for several hours, then drain them. Fry the pork in the olive oil to render the fat, then sauté the onion, carrot, celery, garlic and leek until golden brown. Stir in the tomato paste and cook 2-3 minutes. Add the stocks, bay leaves and red beans and simmer for about 30 minutes. Add the potato and zucchini and return to a simmer.

2 quarts water
1 teaspoon salt
¼ teaspoon white pepper
¼ pound green beans
¼ pound fresh spinach, washed and trimmed
2 cups tubetti pasta, cooked al dente
Grated Parmesan cheese

Bring 2 quarts of water to a boil. Season water with salt and boil the green beans for 5 minutes, then wash them with cold water. In the same boiling water, poach the spinach for 45 seconds. Chop the beans and spinach and add to the soup. Remove pork from the pot and discard. When the potatoes are tender, add the pastetta and the cooked tubetti. Serve in soup bowls, with a sprinkle of Parmesan cheese. Serves 8-10.

Shrimp Bisque Nouvelle

Make no mistake: bisques are beloved in New Orleans, every bit as much as in the Old World of Europe. They are lush, they are rich, they are loaded with flavor. Here's our version of shrimp bisque that's extremely popular whenever we offer it.

¼ cup pure olive oil
1 cup diced white onion
1 cup diced leek
1 cup diced carrot
1 pound shrimp shells
¼ cup tomato paste
½ cup cognac
1 cup white wine
¼ cup flour
1 quart shrimp or fish stock
3 cups water
1 teaspoon Worcestershire sauce
½ cup heavy cream
Salt and black pepper to taste

Heat the olive oil and sauté the vegetables until caramelized, then add the shrimp shells and cook until they turn pink. Stir in the tomato paste until incorporated, then carefully flame with the cognac. When the flames have subsided, deglaze the pan with the white wine. Mix in the flour to thicken, then add the stock and water. Season with Worcestershire. Simmer for 30 minutes. Purée the bisque in batches in a food processor (yes, shrimp shells and all), then strain through a fine sieve. Return the soup to the pot and stir in the cream. Bring to a boil and serve with an extra drizzle of cognac in each bowl. Serves 6-8.

Pan-Roasted Garlic Soup with Asiago

There was a time when Americans ran away from anything with the word "garlic" in the name, so of course the first generation or two of Italians in this country ran away too. What a difference a few generations can make—not to mention dozens of scientific studies linking garlic to good health and long life. Besides, in a city that gave our world Anne Rice and her thirsty vampires, a little extra protection couldn't hurt.

½ cup pure olive oil
16 whole garlic cloves
1 cup chopped onion
½ cup chopped celery
1 cup chopped leek
2 tablespoons flour
2 cups chicken stock
4 cups beef stock
1 teaspoon salt
1 teaspoon freshly ground black pepper

Heat the olive oil in a large, deep saucepan and "roast" the garlic cloves until golden brown. Stir in the onion, celery and leek, cooking until tender. Stir in the flour to thicken, then the two stocks. Bring the liquid to a boil, season with salt and pepper and simmer to reduce for 45 minutes.

1 cup heavy cream
¼ teaspoon Tabasco pepper sauce
2 cups shredded Asiago cheese

In a separate pot, heat the cream and Tabasco until reduced by half. Add to the soup. Purée in a food processor. Return to the pot and bring to a boil. Remove from the heat and stir in the Asiago. Serves 4-6.

Eggplant Parmigiana Soup Alberto

The flavors of Eggplant Parmigiana have been well-known and well-loved in this country for more than a generation. It struck me one day, though, that no one had ever served me a soup incorporating the same ingredients and therefore the same flavors. This has become a huge hit among my guests.

⅓ cup pure olive oil
3 tablespoons finely chopped white onion
1 tablespoon minced garlic
1 cup minced celery
1 cup finely chopped carrot
1 medium eggplant, sliced, cubed and washed
1 teaspoon crushed red pepper
2 tablespoons tomato paste
1 cup white wine
½ cup all-purpose flour
4 cups chicken stock
5 cups beef stock
2 cups water
2 cups canned crushed tomatoes, with juice
1 tablespoon chopped fresh Italian parsley
1 tablespoon chopped fresh oregano
3 bay leaves
1 tablespoon chopped fresh basil
1 teaspoon salt
½ cup grated Parmesan cheese

Heat the oil in a large pot and caramelize the onion and garlic until golden, then stir in the celery and carrot, cooking just until softened. Add the eggplant and stir until lightly browned. Add the red pepper, tomato paste and white wine. Bring to a boil. Sprinkle in the flour and stir once or twice, then add the stocks and water, stirring until thickened. Add the crushed tomatoes, fresh herbs and salt. Reduce heat and simmer 45 minutes. Serve in bowls sprinkled with Parmesan cheese. Serves 4-6.

Lentil Soup Anacaprese

Who doesn't love lentils? Perhaps only those who haven't tried them in this soup. They are one of the life-sustaining pulses of the entire Mediterranean world, from Italy to Spain in the west and all the way east to Lebanon. You might call this soup "poor people's food," but only if you have no clue what makes people truly rich.

4 slices pancetta, coarsely chopped
½ cup pure olive oil
½ cup chopped white onion
½ cup chopped carrot
½ cup chopped celery
2 tablespoons minced garlic
½ teaspoon crushed red pepper
1 cup red wine
1 pound lentils, washed and drained
½ cup crushed tomatoes, with juice
1 gallon beef stock
½ teaspoon salt
⅛ teaspoon white pepper
1 tablespoon chopped fresh Italian parsley
1 tablespoon chopped fresh oregano
1 bay leaf

Fry the pancetta in the olive oil until lightly browned, then sauté the onion, carrot, celery, garlic and crushed red pepper until caramelized. Add the red wine and bring to a boil, then add the lentils, tomatoes and stock. Season with salt, pepper, parsley, oregano and bay leaf. Return to a boil, then lower heat and simmer until the lentils are tender, about 45 minutes.

Extra-virgin olive oil
Chopped fresh Italian parsley
Grated Parmesan cheese

Remove bay leaf. Serve in bowls, garnished with extra-virgin olive oil, parsley and Parmesan cheese. Serves 8-10.

View from my villa in Anacapri

Pasta

Ravioli Caprese

If you make the Lobster Ravioli on page 108, you will have enough homemade pasta to make a full batch of some other ravioli—or you can make cannelloni, or just about anything else. If you choose to make a different ravioli, this one is one of the biggest sellers at Andrea's. Never underestimate what we've been taught to call "The Power of Cheese." Or, in this case, three types of cheese.

Fresh pasta sheets for 36 ravioli

Prepare the pasta sheets as for Lobster Ravioli (page 108).

1 cup shredded mozzarella
1 cup cacciota or ricotta
5 tablespoons grated Parmesan
1 tablespoon minced garlic
2 teaspoons finely chopped white onion
2 egg yolks, lightly beaten
2 tablespoons chopped fresh Italian parsley
2 tablespoons chopped fresh basil
1½ teaspoons marjoram
¼ teaspoon salt
¼ teaspoon white pepper
¼ teaspoon ground nutmeg

In a bowl, make the filling by combining the cheeses, egg yolks, herbs and spices. Fill the ravioli with a spoonful each, then cover with pasta and trim off excess.

Sauce:
3 cups Tomato Basil Sauce (see page 21)
1 tablespoon chopped fresh basil
1 tablespoon unsalted butter
2 tablespoons Parmesan cheese
Fresh basil leaves for garnish

Purée the Tomato Basil Sauce through a food mill into a saucepan and stir in the basil and butter. Cook the ravioli in a large pot of boiling water, about 3-4 minutes until silky-smooth. Toss ravioli in heated sauce with Parmesan cheese. Serve in bowls with sauce, garnished with fresh basil leaves and extra Parmesan cheese. Serves 6 as appetizer, 4 as entrée.

Lobster Ravioli

Here's a lush and elegant pasta dish that's actually a lush and elegant soup in disguise—what serves as the sauce here is actually a classic lobster bisque, a favorite around French New Orleans for generations. In this application, though, the best of Italy makes sure you take notice as well.

Fresh Pasta:

2 cups all-purpose flour
2 cups semolina
2 eggs
1 cup water
1 teaspoon pure olive oil
½ teaspoon salt

Combine the flour and semolina in a large bowl and make a well in the center. Lightly beat the eggs into the water, then stir in the olive oil and salt. Gradually pour this liquid into the well and mix with a fork until all the flour-semolina mix is incorporated. On a clean, dry surface, tear off pieces of the dough and knead by hand for 5 minutes until smooth and elastic. Cover the dough in a bowl and let rest for 5 minutes.

Sauce:

2 (1¼-1½ pound) Maine lobsters,
boiled in salted water and chilled

Break open the lobsters, reserving the heads and tail flippers for garnish. Set the meat aside to make the filling.

½ cup vegetable oil
1 cup roughly chopped onion
1 cup roughly chopped celery
1 cup roughly chopped carrot
1 tablespoon minced garlic
¼ cup tomato paste
¼ cup cognac
½ cup white wine
½ cup all-purpose flour
8 cups water
1 tablespoon chopped fresh thyme
½ cup chopped fresh leek
3 bay leaves
2 teaspoons salt
¼ teaspoon crushed red pepper
1 tablespoon Worcestershire sauce
1 cup heavy cream
¼ teaspoon Tabasco pepper sauce
1 teaspoon salt

In a deep pan, heat the vegetable oil over medium-high heat, then stir in the onion, celery, carrot and garlic until caramelized. Add the lobster shells and stir for 3-4 minutes. Stir in the tomato paste for about 2 minutes, then carefully flame the mixture with cognac. When flame burns out, add the wine and flour, stirring to thicken the liquid. Add the water, along with the thyme, leek, bay leaves, salt, crushed red pepper and Worcestershire. Bring to a boil, then simmer for 45 minutes.

Complete the sauce by puréeing in a large blender or food processor, lobster shells and all. Strain into a pan and stir in cream, Tabasco and salt.

(continued on next page)

Filling:
1 tablespoon unsalted butter
2 tablespoons chopped white onion
1 teaspoon minced garlic
¼ cup chopped leek
½ teaspoon saffron threads
¼ teaspoon paprika
¼ cup cognac
¼ teaspoon Worcestershire sauce
2 drops Tabasco pepper sauce
½ cup white wine
½ cup unseasoned breadcrumbs
¼ cup chopped sun-dried tomatoes
2 tablespoons chopped fresh Italian parsley
¼ teaspoon salt
4 tablespoons shredded mozzarella cheese
2 tablespoons ricotta cheese
1 egg yolk, lightly beaten
2 tablespoons grated Parmesan cheese

2 beaten eggs for brushing

Finely chop the lobster meat. In a sauté pan, melt the butter and sauté the onion and garlic until caramelized, then stir in the leek for a moment. Add the chopped lobster meat. Add the saffron and paprika. Carefully flame the mixture with cognac. When flames subside, add the Worcestershire, Tabasco and white wine. Bring to a boil, then remove from heat, let cool a few minutes and mix in all remaining filling ingredients.

Using a pasta machine, press the dough through in batches 4-5 times to strengthen until you end up with long, thin sheets. Lay one end of these sheets across a ravioli mold so other half can fold back to serve as top. Open the sheet and brush with beaten egg. Fill each ravioli with a spoonful of the stuffing, then cover with the top layer and press down. Use a roller to cut off excess pasta, and reuse. Turn the ravioli out onto a clean, floured surface, cut apart with a sharp knife and press edges closed with fingers. Set on parchment dusted with semolina. Makes 36 ravioli.

Cook the ravioli in generous amounts of boiling water, being careful not to overcrowd. Drain and transfer to large skillet or sauté pan, coating with some of the sauce. Serve in bowls, spooning sauce over the top. Garnish with lobster head and tail flippers and fresh thyme. Serves 6 as an appetizer, 4 as an entrée.

Mamma Regina making gnocchi

Gnocchi Emiliana

Here's one of Italy's greatest (and most different) pasta dishes, in which the pasta itself is made not from semolina flour but from potatoes pressed through a food mill. In the process of making these classic gnocchi (don't worry, you'll get the hang of it quickly!), you'll also get to discover one of the classic Italian sauces, pancetta browned in butter with garlic and fresh sage. And by the way, once you get into the motion, this recipe actually makes about 300 gnocchi. Freeze the ones you don't cook the first time—next time, you'll have a significant head start.

Gnocchi:
3 pounds Idaho potatoes
½ teaspoon ground nutmeg
2 tablespoons softened unsalted butter
1 teaspoon salt
2 egg yolks, lightly beaten
3 cups all-purpose flour

Boil the potatoes until they are tender, 35-40 minutes, then peel off the skins while they are still hot. Cut the potatoes in quarters and set in a preheated 400° oven for 8-10 minutes, to remove excess moisture. Press the potatoes through a food mill set on medium-large (or pulse in a food processor). In a bowl, combine the potatoes with the nutmeg, the butter and the salt. Incorporate the egg yolks one at a time, mixing with a wooden spoon or spatula. Mix in the flour, kneading with your hands to form a thick, elastic dough.

To form the gnocchi, generously flour a clean flat surface and roll out pieces of dough with your hands to form long (3-foot) tubes. Using a knife or pastry cutter, cut these tubes into half-inch lengths. Roll each length into ribbed gnocchi, forming them and scoring them with a fork. Cook the gnocchi in batches in boiling water and remove to a platter, retaining the pasta water.

Sauce:
4 tablespoons butter
1 cup chopped pancetta
2 tablespoons minced garlic
2 tablespoons chopped fresh sage
2 teaspoons salt
¼ teaspoon white pepper
¼ teaspoon ground nutmeg

In a large pan, melt the butter and sauté the pancetta until golden brown. Add the garlic and chopped sage. Add 1 cup of pasta water to enrich the sauce, followed by the salt, white pepper and nutmeg.

2 tablespoons butter
4 tablespoons grated Parmesan
Fresh sage leaves

Transfer the cooked gnocchi to the sauce pan, adding the additional 1 tablespoon butter and the Parmesan cheese. Divide into 8 bowls and garnish with fresh sage leaves. Serves 8.

Spinach-Ricotta Gnocchi with Fresh Tomato Sauce

Now that you have your gnocchi-making technique perfected, I thought I might show you a variation that's delicious in its own right. In this recipe, the gnocchi themselves take on great flavor from the ricotta and spinach, thus telling us the sauce should be simple and rather light. And learning about that kitchen truth might be every bit as important as learning how to make wonderful gnocchi.

Gnocchi:
7 ounces fresh spinach, blanched and drained
2 pounds potatoes, boiled and peeled
2 tablespoons melted butter
¼ teaspoon nutmeg
2 egg yolks, lightly beaten
1 cup flour
2 cups ricotta cheese

Put the spinach and potatoes through a grinder separately, then combine thoroughly in a mixing bowl. Stir in the butter, nutmeg, egg yolks and flour, then turn out onto a floured surface. Using your fingers, knead in the ricotta until you have a firm dough. Roll the dough into long cigars and cut into ½-inch-long gnocchi. Roll each over the tines of a fork to stripe. Cook in batches in plenty of boiling salted water, until the gnocchi float to the top. Strain, reserving pasta water.

Fresh Tomato Sauce:
¼ cup pure olive oil
2 tablespoons chopped white onion
1 tablespoon minced garlic
4 cups chopped tomatoes, with juice
¼ cup chopped fresh basil
1 teaspoon chopped fresh oregano
1 teaspoon salt
1 cup pasta water
3 tablespoons unsalted butter
4 tablespoons grated Parmesan cheese

Heat the olive oil in a large skillet and sauté the onion and garlic until caramelized. Add the tomatoes and bring to a boil. Add the basil, oregano and salt; simmer for 15 minutes. Puree the thickened sauce in a food mill or processor, then return to heat. Add 1 cup of the pasta water and simmer. Toss the gnocchi in the sauce. Stir in the butter and Parmesan cheese. Divide into pasta bowls. Serves 8.

Linguine ai Frutti di Mare

Few things are as true to my island of Capri as fresh pasta tossed with a wide variety of some of the freshest seafood you'll taste anywhere. Such notions made my transition to New Orleans quite a natural, considering all the wonders that arrive in my kitchen every day from the Gulf of Mexico, the bays and the bayous. The idea is always to use what's freshest, what most delivers the mild, clean, wonderful taste of the sea.

⅓ cup extra-virgin olive oil
1 tablespoon chopped white onion
1 tablespoon minced garlic
12 littleneck clams
12 mussels, debearded
½ cup dry white wine
12 cherry tomatoes
1 cup cleaned and chopped calamari
1 cup shelled sea scallops
1 tablespoon chopped Italian parsley
1 tablespoon chopped fresh oregano
1 teaspoon salt
½ teaspoon crushed red pepper

Heat the oil in a large pan and sauté the onion and garlic until caramelized. Add the clams and mussels along with the white wine, cover and let steam. (Discard any that do not open.) Transfer the steamed shellfish to a separate pot filled with salt water, to remove any sand. Squeeze the cherry tomatoes through your fingers into the clam-mussel cooking liquid. Add the calamari and scallops, along with the Italian parsley, oregano, salt and crushed red pepper. Bring to a boil.

8 jumbo shrimp, peeled and deveined
1 cup jumbo lump crabmeat
1 cup Louisiana crawfish tails
¾ pound fresh linguine
Extra-virgin olive oil
Italian parsley for garnish

Add the shrimp, crabmeat and crawfish tails. Return the cleaned clams and mussels to the pot. Cook the linguine al dente in plenty of salted water, then drain it and toss with additional olive oil. Divide the linguine into bowls and top with seafood, making sure each person gets all types. Ladle broth generously into the bowls. Garnish with Italian parsley. Serves 4.

Lasagna Regina

Among home cooks, it's hard to think of a more popular Italian dish than lasagna, Sadly, with all the frozen lasagnas available in the supermarket these days, some of us are forgetting the wonderful freshness of homemade. This recipe—named after my mother, which ought to tell you something—is my argument for always making your own lasagna.

Stuffing:

1 pound ground beef
1½ tablespoons minced garlic
¼ cup chopped onions
2 tablespoons chopped fresh Italian parsley
1 tablespoon chopped fresh oregano
1 tablespoon chopped fresh basil
1 teaspoon salt
¼ teaspoon white pepper
¼ cup grated Parmesan cheese
¼ cup breadcrumbs

Form the stuffing by combining all ingredients in a mixing bowl or food processor then shaping into small meatballs. Bake the meatballs for about 5 minutes in a preheated 400° oven, until light brown.

8 sheets (6-by-18 inch) pasta dough
1 pound fresh spinach, washed and trimmed of stems

Cook the pasta sheets al dente in a large pot of boiling water. Remove from water, wash with cold water and drain. Poach the spinach for 2 minutes in boiling water, then drain and finely chop.

1 tablespoon pure olive oil
2 quarts Tomato Basil Sauce (recipe p. 21)
3 cups ricotta cheese
7 cups shredded mozzarella
3 cups grated Parmesan cheese

Coat the bottom of a large baking pan with olive oil and cover with a layer of pasta, then the Tomato Basil Sauce. Layer on about a third of the meatballs, 1 cup of ricotta, 2 cups of mozzarella, 1 cup of Parmesan, and ¼ cup of spinach. Repeat the sequence 2 more times. Top with the remaining cup of mozzarella.

Place the lasagna pan inside a larger pan half-filled with water and set them in a preheated 450° oven for 30 minutes. Lower heat to 350° and bake an additional 10 minutes. Allow the lasagna to cool for 15 minutes to set before serving. Serve with Tomato Basil Sauce spooned over top. Serves 10-12.

Rigatoni Kevin Bennett

If you like rather intense sauces on your pasta—you know, the kind that turn up more in southern Italy and Sicily than in the Europeanized north—here's a dish named after one of our great customers designed just for you. The anchovies and sun-dried tomatoes make this rigatoni almost jump off the plate, in the general direction of your mouth.

8 cups cooked rigatoni (cooking water reserved)

Cook the rigatoni and reserve 1½ cups of the water for the sauce.

½ cup pure olive oil
½ cup chopped white onion
1 tablespoon minced garlic
⅓ cup white wine
16 cherry tomatoes
⅓ cup finely chopped anchovies
½ cup thinly sliced sun-dried tomatoes
2 tablespoons chopped fresh oregano
½ cup chopped fresh basil
¼ teaspoon crushed red pepper

Heat the olive oil in a large skillet and sauté the onion and garlic until caramelized, then pour in the white wine and cook until evaporated. With your fingers, squeeze the tomatoes and their juice into the pan. Stir in the anchovies, sun-dried tomatoes, oregano and crushed red pepper. Add 1½ cups of the pasta water and let the sauce simmer until slightly thickened.

½ cup softened unsalted butter
2 tablespoons chopped fresh Italian parsley
½ cup grated Parmesan cheese

Toss the cooked rigatoni in the sauce. Stir in the butter and parsley, then remove the pan from the heat and stir in the Parmesan. Divide the rigatoni into pasta bowls. Garnish with thinly sliced basil leaves and additional Parmesan. Serves 4.

Scampi Genovese with Linguine

Genoa was not only the birthplace of Christopher Columbus (I mean Cristoforo Columboo, of course!), but of something that's changed the world just about as much. That's right, pesto sauce. Here's a pasta dish with shrimp that makes the most of the Genovese contribution to western civilization.

Pesto Sauce:
1 cup finely chopped fresh basil
1 tablespoon chopped onion
1 teaspoon chopped garlic
1 stick unsalted butter, softened
½ cup pure olive oil
¼ cup grated Parmesan cheese
¼ cup toasted pinenuts
½ teaspoon salt
4 teaspoon white pepper
¼ cup Italian parsley

To prepare the pesto, pulse the basil in a food processor, then add the onion and garlic and puree. Set aside. Process half the butter, then half the olive oil, then repeat until you have a thickened liquid. Pour this into the basil mixture and add the remaining ingredients. Stir well until smooth.

¼ cup pure olive oil
1 tablespoon chopped white onion
1 teaspoon minced garlic
¼ teaspoon crushed red pepper
24 large shrimp, peeled
⅓ cup white wine
½ cup heavy cream
½ teaspoon salt
½ teaspoon freshly ground black pepper
1 tablespoon Worcestershire sauce

Heat the olive oil in a large skillet and sauté the onion, garlic and crushed red pepper until caramelized. Add the shrimp and sauté just until pink. Pour in the wine and let it evaporate, then add the cream and the pesto sauce. Season with salt, pepper and Worcestershire. Stir together and simmer for 5 minutes, until thickened.

1 pound linguine, cooked al dente
Fresh basil leaves

In another pan, toss the linguine with some of the sauce. Serve in pasta bowls, topped with shrimp and remaining sauce. Garnish with basil leaves. Serves 4.

Penne Arrabiata Dr. Charles Mary

I know we chefs can get a little hot under the collar in the kitchen, but that's nothing compared to this now-famous "Angry Penne." The sauce gets some heat from the crushed red pepper—and as with most things, you can make it as hot as you like just by adding more. I think this penne is the perfect counterpoint to a well-seasoned Italian sausage, which you'll notice goes both in the pasta and on the side.

4 links good-quality Italian sausage
¼ cup pure olive oil
¼ cup chopped white onion
1 tablespoon minced garlic
1 teaspoon crushed red pepper
½ cup red wine
1 tablespoon chopped fresh basil
1 tablespoon chopped fresh oregano
1 teaspoon salt
1 teaspoon freshly ground black pepper
2 small bay leaves
1 cup beef stock
4 cups crushed tomato

Remove the casings from 2 of the Italian sausage links and chop up stuffing. Heat the olive oil in a large skillet and sauté the onion and garlic until caramelized. Add the crushed red pepper with the chopped sausage and stir until browned. Pour in the wine and let evaporate, followed by the basil, oregano, salt, pepper, bay leaves and beef stock. Poke a few holes in the remaining sausage links and place in the pot with the sausage, then cover with the crushed tomato. Cover and cook for 15 minutes. Remove the sausage links and slice diagonally. Remove the bay leaves.

1 pound penne, cooked al dente
Grated Parmesan cheese

Toss the cooked penne with the sauce. Serve in bowls, topped with sliced sausage and the remaining sauce. Sprinkle with Parmesan cheese. Serves 4.

Rigatoni Norma

Here's one of Italy's classic pasta and eggplant combinations—almost certainly named after the famous opera by Bellini. We don't remember Norma herself eating any pasta in that opera, but that's okay. Your guests will eat enough for her. And playing some Bellini in the background (or sipping some Bellinis before dinner!) would be just fine too.

1 cup pure olive oil
4 whole cloves garlic
1 medium eggplant, cut in squares

Heat the olive oil in a large pan and sauté the garlic cloves until golden. Add the eggplant and sauté in batches until medium-dark brown around the edges, about 5 minutes. Drain on paper towels and reserve the oil.

4 cups crushed Italian plum tomatoes, with juice
½ cup chopped fresh basil
2 sprigs fresh oregano, chopped
3 cups rigatoni, coked al dente
1 tablespoon extra-virgin olive oil
1 teaspoon salt
1 teaspoon white pepper
Grated Parmesan cheese
½ cup Pecorino cheese
½ cup ricotta cheese

In the reserved olive oil, bring the tomatoes to a boil and add the basil and oregano. Simmer until the sauce is reduced by about half, about 5 minutes. Return the eggplant to the pan and remove from heat. Toss the cooked rigatoni in the extra-virgin olive oil, then toss with about half the sauce. Serve rigatoni in bowls, with remaining sauce spooned over top. Sprinkle with the Parmesan and Pecorino; crumble on the ricotta. Serves 4-6.

Crawfish Sidney with Angel Hair

Sidney Lassen has been one of my very best customers for 30 years, going back to my first days in New Orleans at the Royal Orleans Hotel. I cook now for his children and grandchildren. Over those years, I've created a lot of different dishes in his honor and, of course, for his guests in my restaurant. But I think this is one of the dishes most worthy of his name. By the way, Sidney agrees.

⅓ cup unsalted butter
2 tablespoons chopped shallot
2 teaspoons minced garlic
4 cups Louisiana crawfish tails, with fat
1 cup vodka
2 cups heavy cream
½ teaspoon salt
½ teaspoon freshly ground black pepper
¼ teaspoon crushed red pepper
1 teaspoon Worcestershire sauce

Melt the butter in a skillet and sauté the shallots and garlic until caramelized, then add the crawfish tails and sauté. Carefully flame with the vodka, then when the flames subside, pour in the cream. Bring to a boil to reduce until thickened. Season with salt, pepper, crushed red pepper and Worcestershire sauce.

4 cups cooked angel hair pasta
Fresh dill weed or Italian parsley leaves

Toss the cooked angel hair with some of the crawfish and sauce, then serve in bowls with remaining sauce spooned over top. Garnish with Italian parsley. Serves 4.

Risotto Milanese

You can't say this too often: in the north of Italy, risotto made with Arborio rice and polenta made with cornmeal are enjoyed every bit as often (and every bit as authentically) as any pasta. In those regions, when people talk about having a little pasta every day, they are probably including risotto and polenta in their definition.

2 tablespoons pure olive oil
2 tablespoons chopped white onion
1 teaspoon minced garlic
2 cups Arborio rice
½ teaspoon saffron threads
½ cup white wine
3 cups chicken stock
¼ cup unsalted butter

Heat the olive oil in a saucepan and sauté the onion and garlic until caramelized. Stir in the rice and the saffron threads, until rice has browned slightly. Pour in the wine to evaporate, followed by the chicken stock. Bring to a boil, add ¼ cup butter and transfer to a preheated 400° oven until rice is cooked al dente, about 10 minutes.

2 tablespoons grated Parmesan cheese
1 tablespoon unsalted butter

Stir in the Parmesan and the butter. Serves 6.

Risotto Bianco

Though similar in technique to Risotto Milanese, this version provides an even blander underpinning for an even more delicate seafood dish. Without the saffron and cheese, it is a light, subtle starch that's perfect when the idea of "white rice" seems best.

⅓ cup pure olive oil
1 tablespoon chopped onion
1 teaspoon minced garlic
½ cup white wine
2 cups Arborio rice
3 cups fish stock
1 teaspoon salt
⅓ cup unsalted butter

Heat the olive oil and lightly sauté the onion and garlic, then pour in the wine to evaporate. Add the rice and stir over heat for 1-2 minutes, then add the fish stock, salt and butter. Transfer to a preheated 400° oven until rice is cooked al dente, about 10 minutes. Drizzle with extra-virgin olive oil. Serves 6.

After-Hours Angel Hair Salvatore

This is the name we give to a pasta dish we love to throw together late at night, maybe after a movie or a play or maybe after a football game, when no one has enough energy to cook something complicated. It really is as simple as it seems; but like most things in Italian cooking, simplicity ends up equaling flavor.

2 pounds fresh angel hair pasta
¼ cup pure olive oil
4 cloves garlic, smashed
18 cherry tomatoes
4 sprigs fresh Italian parsley, chopped
12 fresh basil leaves, chopped
¼ teaspoon salt
¼ teaspoon black pepper
¼ teaspoon crushed red pepper
¼ cup grated Parmesan cheese
Extra-virgin olive oil

Cook the pasta quickly in boiling salted water, 2-3 minutes. Drain, reserving ¾ cup of the pasta water. Heat the oil in a large skillet and caramelize the smashed garlic. Crush the tomatoes over the garlic, then stir in the parsley and basil. Season with salt, pepper and crushed red pepper, along with the reserved pasta water. Bring to a boil. Add the cooked pasta and toss quickly. Serve sprinkled with Parmesan cheese and drizzled with olive oil. Serves 4.

Note: For an even quicker version of this sauce, go for traditional *aglio e olie*—this recipe without tomatoes or basil.

View of Bagni Tiberio from Anacapri

Pesce

Recipe on page 129

Sogliola alla Mugnaia

At Andrea's, we fly in our fresh sole directly from Dover on the English Channel, a clear tribute to its favor among all the fish in the sea. Preparing it *alla mugnaia* is our version of the French "brown butter" meuniere so beloved in New Orleans. As in other great Creole dishes, you can brown almonds or pecans in the sauce for extra nutty flavor and lots of extra crunch.

Fish Marinade:
2 tablespoons extra-virgin olive oil
2 tablespoons dry white wine
2 teaspoons freshly squeezed lemon juice
1 teaspoon Worcestershire sauce
¼ teaspoon Tabasco pepper sauce

Mix the marinade in a shallow platter and let each fillet marinate for about 30 seconds on each side.

2 tablespoons pure olive oil
4 Dover sole fillets

Heat the olive oil in the skillet and sauté the fish until lightly browned on one side. Turn onto a baking pan and set the pan in a preheated 400° oven for 5 minutes.

3 tablespoons unsalted butter
2 teaspoons lemon juice
½ cup dry white wine
3-4 drops Tabasco pepper sauce
4-5 drops Worcestershire sauce
½ teaspoon salt
¼ teaspoon white pepper

Melt the butter in the skillet and bring to a bubbling boil. Quickly add the lemon juice, white wine, Tabasco, Worcestershire, salt and pepper. As soon as it starts to bubble, pour the sauce over the sole and serve immediately on dinner plates. Serves 4.

Trota Imperiale

You'll never lose a friend (or a customer!) in New Orleans serving something that involves putting lump crabmeat on top of speckled trout. Though a member of the bass family, rather than a true trout like rainbow, the "spec" is indeed an emperor pulled from local waters. Thus the big deal we make of it here.

Lemon Cream Sauce:
½ cup freshly squeezed lemon juice
½ cup dry white wine
½ teaspoon Worcestershire sauce
3 cups whipping cream
1 teaspoon salt
¼ teaspoon white pepper

Prepare the Lemon Cream sauce, following the directions carefully to keep the lemon from curdling the cream. Combine the lemon juice, wine and Worcestershire in a skillet and reduce by half. Remove from the heat. In a separate skillet, reduce the cream and season with salt and pepper. Whisk the lemon-wine mixture into the cream—don't try it the other way around. Keep the sauce warm while preparing the fish.

Fish Marinade:
(see page 134)
4 speckled trout fillets

Combine the marinade ingredients and marinate the fillets about 1 minute per side.

Salt and freshly ground black pepper
¼ cup all-purpose flour
½ cup vegetable oil

Season with salt and pepper, and dust lightly with flour, shaking off excess. Heat the oil in a large oven-proof skillet and sauté the fillets until lightly browned on one side. Turn them and set the skillet in a preheated 400° oven for 6 minutes.

2 tablespoons butter
1 cup jumbo lump crabmeat

Melt the butter in a separate skillet and sauté the crabmeat about 2 minutes, being careful not to break up the lumps. Gently incorporate the Lemon Cream sauce. Serve the trout with sauce spooned over the top. Serves 4.

(Pictured on page 127)

Seared Tuna Puttanesca

This intense sauce, a bit infamous over spaghetti because of its association with ladies of the evening, is actually one of the best toppings I know for wonderful seared fresh tuna. Use the best tuna you can get your hands on, because I like my tuna no more cooked than medium rare. And yes, if you're feeling a little devilish, you can always serve the extra sauce over spaghetti!

2 tablespoons extra-virgin olive oil
⅓ cup chopped white onion
1 tablespoon minced garlic
½ teaspoon crushed red pepper
¼ cup chopped and crushed anchovies
4 cups crushed tomatoes
¼ cup capers
2 tablespoons chopped fresh oregano
1 tablespoon chopped fresh Italian parsley
1 tablespoon chopped fresh basil
1 teaspoon salt

Heat the extra-virgin olive oil in a deep skillet and sauté the onion until caramelized, then add the garlic and cook just until golden. Add the crushed red pepper, anchovies, tomatoes and capers. Using your fingers, crush the olives into the sauce. Add the oregano, Italian parsley, basil and salt. Bring to a boil, then simmer over low heat for 25 minutes.

6 (6-8 ounce) tuna steaks
Salt and black pepper
2 tablespoons pure olive oil

Season the tuna with salt and pepper. Sear in the olive oil about 1 minute per side, then set in a preheated 425° oven for 5 minutes. Serve tuna on dinner plates, with sauce divided over the top and sides. Serves 6.

Grilled Sea Bass with Salsa a la Minuta

Here's the perfect fish dish for anyone who hates covering up the freshest seafood with some highly developed French-style sauce. The words "a la minuta" say it all—a sauce so easy, quick and light you can swirl it together while the fish is passing briefly through your oven. But oh, this short-on-time favorite definitely won't be short on flavor.

4 (8-ounce) sea bass fillets

Grill the sea bass fillets on a preheated grill for 2 minutes, then turn for 1½ minutes, for "striping" on both sides. Transfer grilled fillets to a skillet with a little water and set in preheated 425° oven for 7-8 minutes.

Sautéed Spinach:
3 tablespoons pure olive oil
3 teaspoons minced garlic
4 cups fresh spinach leaves
¼ teaspoon crushed red pepper
¼ cup chicken stock
Salt and freshly ground black pepper to taste

Meanwhile, heat the olive oil in a pan and sauté the garlic until caramelized. Add the spinach, red pepper and chicken stock, cooking until barely wilted. Season to taste with salt and pepper and divide onto 4 dinner plates.

Salsa a la Minuta:
½ cup pure olive oil
½ cup extra-virgin olive oil
Salt and crushed red pepper to taste
2 teaspoons chopped fresh oregano
2 teaspoons chopped fresh basil
1 teaspoon minced garlic
1 teaspoon finely chopped onion
1 tablespoon capers
2 Roma tomatoes, chopped
¼ cup white wine
1 teaspoon freshly squeezed lemon juice

Combine all ingredients in a bowl. Remove the sea bass from the oven and carefully set each fillet atop a mound of spinach. Spoon the salsa over the top. Serves 4.

Sautéed Snapper Acqua Pazza

One of our guests' long-time favorite dishes is this one strangely named "crazy water." The sauce is incredibly light but also incredibly flavorful. Maybe the only thing really crazy about this recipe is how crazy your guests will be to have you cook it again and again. Then you'll know how I feel!

1 tablespoon chopped fresh Italian parsley
1 tablespoon chopped fresh oregano
1 teaspoon crushed red pepper
¼ teaspoon salt
4 (8-ounce) red snapper or other firm, white-fleshed fish fillets
4 tablespoons pure olive oil
4 cloves garlic, thinly sliced

In a bowl, combine the parsley, oregano, red pepper and salt, then spread this mixture onto both sides of the snapper fillets, pressing it in lightly. Heat the olive oil in a sauté pan until very hot, then briefly sauté the fish on both sides. Add the garlic to caramelize. Transfer the fish to a preheated 425° oven for 7-8 minutes.

1 Roma tomato, chopped
1 cup dry white wine
1 cup fish stock

In the sauté pan, combine the tomato, wine and fish stock, heating until it bubbles. Serve the fillets on warmed dinner plates, with a generous ¼ cup of sauce ladled over each. Serves 4.

Softshell Crab Basilico

One of the great joys of life along the Gulf Coast has got to be soft-shell crabs—especially since they are available now almost every day of the year. This recipe marinates the crabs, then lightly sautés them, then showcases them with a sprightly sauce.

Marinade:
2 tablespoons freshly squeezed lemon juice
2 tablespoons white wine
1 tablespoon Worcestershire sauce
8 drops Tabasco pepper sauce
Salt and freshly ground black pepper

⅓ cup pure olive oil
4 large soft-shell crabs
2 tablespoons all-purpose flour

1 tablespoon pure olive oil
1 tablespoon chopped white onion
1 teaspoon minced garlic
2 Roma tomatoes, chopped
⅓ cup white wine
1 cup fish stock
1 cup sliced mushrooms
Juice of 1 lemon
¼ teaspoon Tabasco pepper sauce
1 tablespoon capers
½ teaspoon salt
¼ cup unsalted butter
¼ cup chopped fresh basil

Combine the marinade ingredients and pour over the soft-shell crabs. Marinate for 5 minutes, turning the crabs in the liquid. Season with salt and pepper.

Heat the olive oil in a large skillet. Dust the crabs with flour and brown on all sides, then set skillet in a preheated 400° oven until crabs are firm to the touch, 5-7 minutes.

In a separate pan, heat the 1 tablespoon of olive oil and sauté the onion and garlic until golden, then stir in the tomatoes. Add the white wine and let it evaporate, then pour in the fish stock and all remaining ingredients. Heat thoroughly. Place a soft-shell crab on each plate and spoon the sauce over the top. Serves 4.

Note: This is a wonderful sauce for sautéed redfish, red snapper or speckled trout.

Spiedini di Pesce Spada Taormina

I know you've had shish kebab before but quite possibly nothing like this luscious seafood rendition from deep in the Mediterranean world. Don't ever forget that the world's finest swordfish brush right up against Sicily while making their regular inspection tours, and Sicilian fisherman love it when they do. This dish is great cooked at home, but even greater cooked over an open fire on the beach near Taormina!

Stuffing:

1 cup breadcrumbs
⅓ cup chopped white onion
1 tablespoon minced garlic
⅓ cup pinenuts
½ teaspoon crushed red pepper
1 tablespoon chopped fresh oregano
1 tablespoon chopped fresh Italian pasley
1 tablespoon extra-virgin olive oil
4 anchovies, chopped
2 tablespoons Pecorino Romano cheese
4 ounces shredded cacciocavallo cheese

Prepare the stuffing by combining all ingredients in a mixing bowl.

12 thin slices fresh swordfish
1 white onion, quartered and lightly blanched
8 bay leaves
⅓ cup pure olive oil
Salt and black pepper to taste
¼ cup all-purpose flour
Chopped fresh Italian parsley for garnish
Risotto Bianco (recipe p. 124)

Roll about 1 tablespoon of stuffing in each thin slice of swordfish. Thread the swordfish 3 to a skewer, alternating with slices of blanched onion and bay leaves. Heat the olive oil in a skillet. Season the skewers with salt and pepper and dust with flour, shaking off excess. Brown the spiedini in the hot oil. Remove from the pan.

Sauce:

1 tablespoon minced garlic
½ cup white wine
1 tablespoon chopped fresh oregano
1 cup finely chopped tomato with juice
1 cup fish stock

In the pan drippings, prepare the sauce by heating the oil and caramelizing the garlic. Add the white wine and let it evaporate, then add all remaining ingredients. Set skewers in the sauce and place pan in a preheated 425° oven for 8-10 minutes, turning them halfway through. Season to taste with salt and pepper. Unskewer onto dinner plates. Spoon sauce over the top and sides. Serve with Risotto Bianco. Garnish with Italian parsley. Serves 4.

Spiedini di Mare with Saffron Cream Sauce

Once you've perfected your skewering technique making those swordfish kebabs, you might try your hand at spiedini graduate school. No, it's not really much harder. But the tastes and textures are a bit more diverse. Plus, your guests are sure to love just about anything you serve them with this ultra-lush saffron cream sauce.

Saffron Cream Sauce:
¼ cup unsalted butter
2 tablespoons all-purpose flour
⅓ cup white wine
2 cups fish stock
1 tablespoon pure olive oil
1 teaspoon minced garlic
¼ teaspoon saffron threads
1 cup heavy cream
1 teaspoon Worcestershire sauce
2 drops Tabasco pepper sauce
¼ teaspoon salt

Melt the butter in a skillet. Stir in the flour and wine, whisking until smooth. Incorporate the fish stock. Bring to a boil until thickened, then keep at a simmer. In a separate pan, heat the olive oil and sauté the garlic until it's caramelized. Stir in the saffron and cream. Reduce until thickened and simmer. Strain the white sauce into the yellow sauce and stir to combine. Add the Worcestershire, Tabasco and salt. Keep warm.

Spiedini:
8 thick slices pancetta or bacon
8 (21-25 count) shrimp, peeled
1 red bell pepper
8 leeks, poached
8 sea scallops
1 poached onion, cut in chunks
4 bay leaves
Salt and freshly ground black pepper
⅓ cup pure olive oil

Make the spiedini by wrapping the pancetta around the shrimp. Roast the bell pepper until charred, then peel away the black outer layer and chop what remains. Wrap the leeks around the scallops. Carefully skewer one scallop, one roasted pepper, one shrimp, one poached onion and one bay leaf, then repeat sequence. Do all 4 skewers this way. Season with salt and pepper.

In a large sauté pan, heat the olive oil. Sear the skewers in the hot oil, turning until all sides are flecked with brown. Turn for about 5 minutes, then set the pan in a preheated 400° oven until golden, about 7 minutes. Unskewer the seafood onto dinner plates and spoon saffron cream sauce over top and sides. Serves 4-6.

Salt-Crusted Redfish with Salsetta

Not many diners, it seems, know about crusting fresh fish with salt to preserve both moisture and flavor, and even fewer have dared to try it at home. Like so many things in the kitchen, it is easier and less exotic than it looks. Considering the depth of commitment demanded of the redfish, we believe he'd be glad you treated him with such respect.

1 (2-3 pound) redfish, head and tail on, cleaned
Salt
4 sprigs fresh mint
2 sprigs fresh rosemary

Salt the whole fish and brown on both sides over a flat grill or in a preheated 400° oven, turning the fish once. Remove the fish and fill the cavity with mint and rosemary.

4 egg whites
2 cups salt
1 cup cornstarch

In a bowl, whip the egg whites until thick and foamy, then stir in the salt and cornstarch. With a spatula, spread the white mixture over the top of the fish in the roasting pan, making sure it covers all sides. Set in the oven for 45 minutes. When cooked, remove the hardened salt crust by tapping with a knife and peeling away.

Salsetta:
¼ cup pure olive oil
¼ cup extra-virgin olive oil
1 teaspoon minced garlic
¼ cup white wine
1 tablespoon chopped fresh Italian parsley
1 tablespoon chopped fresh mint
½ teaspoon crushed red pepper
Juice of 1 lemon
½ teaspoon salt

Quickly prepare the salsetta by combining all ingredients in a bowl. Cut into the fish and debone, transferring the moist, flavorful flesh to a decorative platter. Spoon salsetta over the fish and serve. Serves 4-6.

Summer Avocado, Shrimp and Crabmeat Salad

Yes, it gets hot in New Orleans in the summertime, as it does in many parts of Italy. Along the coasts of both places, there's a happy tendency to incorporate chilled fresh seafood into as many meals as possible. We think you'll find this simple salad perfect for a summer lunch and, well—way cool!

2 avocados
Mixed baby greens
½ cup sliced mushrooms
8 black olives
½ cup chopped Roma tomatoes
8 boiled shrimp, peeled
1 cup lump crabmeat
Balsamic vinaigrette
Lemon wedges

Slice the avocados in half and spoon out the center. Set them on salad plates of mixed greens. In a bowl, combine the mushrooms, olives and tomatoes. Gently fold in the shrimp and crabmeat. Fill the avocados and drizzle with balsamic vinaigrette or your favorite salad dressing. Garnish with lemon wedges and additional thin slices of avocado. Serves 4.

Lido del Fao, Anacapri

Carne

Recipe on page 168

Buffalo Sirloin Strip with Forest Mushrooms

Buffalo—or more accurately, bison, so Buffalo Bill should really be called Bison Bill—is one of the healthiest meats we have available to us. It's high in nutrients but incredibly low in fat. Because of this, it can dry out very fast, keeping meat moist being one of the things fat does best. This method of cooking with this wonderful sauce will showcase buffalo, or bison, to its best intent. And while we suggest some favorites, feel free to use whatever forest mushrooms are in season where you are.

½ cup pure olive oil
6 (8-ounce) buffalo sirloin strip steaks
Salt and freshly ground black pepper

Heat the olive oil in a large skillet. Season the steaks with salt and pepper and sear on all sides in the hot oil. Transfer the steaks to a different skillet and place in a preheated 400° oven to reach the desired degree of doneness. Rare or medium rare is probably best, considering the low fat content of the meat.

2 tablespoons chopped shallot
1 teaspoon minced garlic
2 cups fresh chanterelle mushrooms
1 cup fresh black trumpet mushrooms
2 portobello mushrooms, sliced
1 teaspoon chopped fresh rosemary
2 leaves fresh sage, chopped
1 cup red wine
⅓ cup unsalted butter
¼ cup heavy cream
½ teaspoon salt
½ teaspoon freshly ground black pepper

In the original skillet, sauté the shallot and garlic until caramelized, then sauté the mushrooms until they begin to brown. Add the herbs, then pour in the wine, letting the liquid cook down a bit until syrupy. Enrich the sauce with butter and cream, bubbling to reduce and thicken. Season with salt and pepper. Transfer the steaks to dinner plates and spoon the mushrooms and sauce over the top and sides. Serves 6.

Roast Stuffed Leg of Lamb with Mint Sauce

Everybody knows what comes with leg of lamb, right? Mint jelly. But in this Old World recipe, the wonderful contrasting flavor of mint turns up not in jelly but in the delicious red wine sauce. This dish makes a dramatic presentation, a sure sign you care about your guests on any evening you choose to serve it.

Stuffing:

1 pound ground lamb
1 pound ground pork
1 onion, finely chopped
1 whole head of garlic, minced
½ cup chopped fresh Italian parsley
1 sprig rosemary, chopped
Bacon
Salt and black pepper to taste

Form the stuffing in a bowl by combining the ground lamb and pork with all the herbs and spices. Stuff the opening in the lamb leg where the bone was removed. Wrap the leg in strips of bacon and tie closed with twine. Season to taste with salt and pepper.

½ cup pure olive oil
1 (10-12 pound) leg of lamb, deboned by butcher
2 stalks celery, chopped
1 onion, chopped
1 carrot, chopped
3 cloves garlic, minced
1 sprig rosemary, chopped
1 tablespoon tomato paste
1 cup red wine
2 quarts water

Heat the olive oil in a roasting pan and brown the lamb leg on all sides. Chop up the reserved bones to fit and add to the browning process, along with the chopped vegetables. Cook until all are caramelized. Stir in tomato paste and cook about 2 minutes, then add the red wine and scrape the browned bits from the bottom of the pan. Add the water. Set the roasting pan in a preheated 425° oven until the meat is tender, about 1¼ hours.

4 springs fresh mint, finely chopped
Salt and black pepper to taste

Remove the leg from the pan. Take out the bones. Strain the sauce through a fine sieve. Purée the vegetables in a food processor and add them back to the strained sauce. Stir in the fresh mint. Season to taste with salt and pepper. Serves 8-10.

Lamb Shank Abruzzi

It's ironic that, while so many restaurants prefer quick-cooked items for obvious reasons of practicality, the heart and soul of rustic Italian cuisine lies in slow-cooked dishes like this. Ours, at best, is a peasant cuisine gone uptown—showing the finesse of "haute" but never losing the deep, rich flavor that comes of simple people cooking what they've grown and raised in the countryside.

1 cup vegetable oil
6 lamb shanks
½ tablespoon salt
½ tablespoon freshly ground black pepper
3 tablespoons all-purpose flour
1 cup pure olive oil
1 cup chopped white onion
1 cup chopped carrot
1 cup chopped celery
2 tablespoons minced garlic
⅓ cup tomato paste
2 cups red wine
½ cup flour
8 cups water
½ teaspoon chopped rosemary
6 fresh mint leaves, chopped

Heat the vegetable oil in a large pot or Dutch oven. Season the lamb shanks with salt and pepper and brown them on all sides in the hot oil. Add any additional bones or meat to the pot to give additional flavor. When dark brown, remove all meat and bones from the pot and add the olive oil to the drippings. Sauté the onion, carrot, celery and garlic until caramelized, then stir in the tomato paste and cook for 2-3 minutes. When mixture is dark brown, add the wine and whisk in the flour until a smooth, burgundy-colored mixture results. Add the water, along with the rosemary and mint. Bring to a boil.

1 teaspoon salt
1 teaspoon pepper
¼ teaspoon crushed red pepper
Whole fresh mint leaves

Return the lamb to the liquid. Season with salt, pepper and crushed red pepper. Transfer the pot to a preheated 425° oven until lamb is fork-tender and sauce is thickened, about 1¼ hours. Garnish with mint leaves and serve with pasta (pictured) or, for a true comfort food, Roasted Garlic Mashed Potatoes.

Roasted Garlic Mashed Potatoes:
1 cup milk
1 cup cream
2 teaspoons salt
10 roasted garlic cloves
1½ pounds potatoes, peeled and boiled
½ cup melted butter
½ teaspoon ground nutmeg

Prepare the mashed potatoes by bringing the milk and cream to a boil in a saucepot, along with the salt and roasted garlic cloves. Remove from heat. Mash the potatoes with a fork or masher, then stir into the milk and cream. Fold in the butter and nutmeg. Serve the lamb shanks with the mashed potatoes, with sauce spooned over both. Garnish with mint leaves. Serves 6.

Osso Buco alla Gremolata Milanese

I'm pleased that osso buco—surely Italy's great contribution to the history of braising meats—has found such a tender place in the hearts of Americans. There are a million variations, of course, using veal, lamb and other shanks. But if you want a dish that will "sell" right off your home-cooking menu, announce your plans to serve osso buco. Here's all there is to making it.

½ cup pure olive oil
6 (1½ inch thick) center-cut veal shanks, tied with twine
1 tablespoon salt
1 cup chopped white onion
1 cup chopped carrot
1 cup chopped celery
1 tablespoon minced garlic
¼ cup tomato paste
2 tablespoons all-purpose flour
1 cup white wine
6 cups chicken stock
4 bay leaves
1 teaspoon chopped fresh rosemary
1 tablespoon salt
½ tablespoon freshly ground black pepper

Zest of 1 lemon
Zest of 1 orange
1 tablespoon chopped fresh Italian parsley
1 teaspoon minced garlic
Risotto Milanese (recipe p. 124)
Rosemary sprigs

Heat the olive oil in a large skillet. Season the shanks with salt and brown them on all sides in the hot oil, about 10 minutes in all. Remove the shanks and, in the pan drippings, sauté the onion, carrot and celery until caramelized, then stir in the garlic until golden. Add the tomato paste and flour, stirring for 2-3 minutes. Add the white wine and cook to evaporate, then pour in the chicken stock. Add the bay leaves, rosemary and salt. Bring to a boil, then cover and transfer to a preheated 400° oven. Cook until meat is fork tender, about 1½ hours. Remove the twine from the shanks.

Make the gremolata by combining the citrus zests with Italian parsley, garlic and a little of the sauce. Serve the osso buco atop Risotto Milanese, with gremolata spooned on top and plenty of sauce around the sides. Serves 6.

Beef Brocioloni Giuseppina

This is one of everybody's favorite Italian beef dishes, with meat made tender by slow cooking rolled around a savory filling and a trademark boiled egg. The sauce of red wine and plum tomatoes, taken on a holiday by all the juices from the meat, is enough to justify many dippings of rustic bread.

Stuffing:

3 ounces Pecorino Romano cheese
4 cloves garlic, minced
½ onion, finely chopped
1 tablespoon pine nuts
1 tablespoon raisins
1 cup breadcrumbs
4 leaves fresh basil, chopped
1 sprig fresh oregano, chopped
1 sprig fresh Italian parsley, chopped
1 tablespoon extra-virgin olive oil

Prepare the stuffing by combining all ingredients in a bowl.

4 (6-ounce) beef top round steaks
Salt and black pepper to taste
2 hard-boiled eggs, cut in half
1 tablespoon pure olive oil
⅓ cup red wine
3 cups crushed tomatoes and juice
1 bay leaf
1 sprig fresh oregano, chopped
2 leaves fresh basil, chopped
Salt and black pepper to taste

Pound out the steaks and season with salt and pepper. Divide the stuffing over the steaks and top with a hard-boiled egg half. Roll up the beef and tie closed with twine. Heat the olive oil in a heavy skillet and brown the meat on all sides. Add the remaining ingredients, bring to a boil and set in a preheated 400° oven until tender, about 45 minutes. Cut away the twine and serve brocioloni with pasta and plenty of sauce. Serves 4.

Veal Paillard with Salsa Verde

There are many dishes from Italy and the rest of the Mediterranean world that demonstrate how people can eat healthy foods and never feel deprived, the way we do so often on our silly "diets" in this country. Here's a dish that's profoundly flavorful yet reflects most of the valid ideas on healthy eating.

Salsa Verde:
1 cup extra-virgin olive oil
¼ cup chopped onion
2 tablespoons minced garlic
1 teaspoon crushed red pepper
1 cup white wine
½ cup freshly squeezed lemon juice
1 teaspoon salt
¼ teaspoon white pepper
1 tablespoon chopped fresh rosemary
1 tablespoon chopped fresh oregano
⅓ cup chopped fresh Italian parsley

To prepare the Salsa Verde, heat the olive oil in a skillet and sauté the onion, garlic and crushed red pepper until caramelized. Then add all remaining sauce ingredients and bring just to a boil. Remove from heat.

¼ cup extra-virgin olive oil
6 (4-ounce) slices veal leg, pounded very thin
Salt and white pepper

To prepare the veal paillards, heat the olive oil very hot in a skillet and sizzle the meat just until brown flecks start to form, then quickly turn in the pan. Total cooking time should be no more than 20-30 seconds. Serve on dinner plates topped with the Salsa Verde. Serves 6.

Veal Tanet

Every once in a while, as a chef, you create a dish that not only becomes a major hit but actually crosses over onto other restaurant menus. That's what happened to Veal Tanet, created during my Royal Orleans days and named after prominent attorney Ronald Tanet. Ronald asked me to make him veal Milanese without the sauce and to serve it with a simple lettuce and tomato salad. Little did he know, everything he wanted that day would come together on a single plate!

Vinaigrette:
¼ cup Dijon mustard
¼ cup white wine vinegar
¼ teaspoon sugar
1 teaspoon cold water
¾ cup extra-virgin olive oil
Salt and white pepper to taste

Prepare the vinaigrette by whisking together the first 4 ingredients, then slowly whisk in the olive oil and season with salt and pepper.

4 (4-ounce) slices veal leg, pounded very thin
Salt and freshly ground black pepper
½ cup all-purpose flour
4 eggs, beaten
3 cups unseasoned breadcrumbs
1 cup vegetable oil

Season the veal with salt and pepper. Dust with flour, shaking off excess, then pass through the beaten egg and bury in the breadcrumbs. Coat well, shaking off excess. Heat the vegetable oil in a large skillet and add each piece of veal very carefully to keep from splashing. Sauté about 1 minute on the first side, then only 30 seconds on the other. Drain the veal on paper towels.

1 head romaine lettuce, washed and dried
2 ripe tomatoes, sliced

Spread romaine leaves over 4 dinner plates and top with tomato slices. Serve the veal atop the tomatoes, with generous spoonfuls of the vinaigrette. Serves 4.

Costolette di Capriolo and Scallopine

This dish comes from the regions of northern Italy that have had the most historic interplay with Austria and Switzerland. People usually think of it as a winter dish—and it certainly is a great one—but I've been known to enjoy it all year round. Have your butcher do as much of the meat trimming and cutting as you can; the work isn't difficult, but it will save you some time. And notice the way I like to sauté the spaetzle noodles until they're golden and crispy. They almost become snack food this way.

Sauce:

2 pounds venison bones
¼ cup vegetable oil
1 cup roughly chopped onion
1 cup roughly chopped celery
1 cup roughly chopped carrot
¼ cup whole garlic cloves
½ tablespoon juniper berries, crushed
½ cup tomato paste
2 cups red wine
½ cup all-purpose flour
8 cups water
4 bay leaves
1 tablespoon chopped fresh rosemary
1 tablespoon chopped fresh thyme
1 tablespoon whole black peppercorns
1 teaspoon salt
1 teaspoon black pepper

To prepare the sauce, brown the bones over high heat in the vegetable oil, then stir in and caramelize the onion, celery, carrot and garlic cloves. Add the juniper berries, then the tomato paste, mixing to brown well. Pour in the wine and scrape the browned bits from the bottom of the pot until the liquid has mostly evaporated. Stir in the flour just until it is cooked, 1-2 minutes. Add the water followed by the bay leaves, rosemary, thyme, peppercorns, salt and pepper. Bring to a boil, then let simmer over medium-low heat for 1½ hours, until the sauce is thick and dark.

Red Cabbage:

2 tablespoons pure olive oil
2 tablespoons pork fat
2 tablespoons chopped white onion
1 teaspoon minced garlic
3 cups shredded red cabbage
½ cup red wine
¼ cup red wine vinegar
1 apple, peeled and grated
1 potato, peeled and grated
1 tablespoon sugar

Prepare the red cabbage by heating the oil and pork fat in an ovenproof skillet and stirring the onion and garlic until caramelized. Briefly sauté the shredded cabbage, then add the red wine and the vinegar, cooking until the liquid is mostly evaporated. Add the shredded apple and set in a preheated 425° oven for about 10 minutes, then add the grated potato and return to the oven for 20-25 minutes. Stir in the sugar for a traditional sweet and sour effect. Keep warm.

(continued on next page)

Spaetzle:

4 cups all-purpose flour
¼ teaspoon salt
1 tablespoon pure olive oil
3 eggs, beaten
1 cup water
½ teaspoon ground nutmeg
Boiling water

Make the spaetzle by combining the flour with the salt and olive oil in the bowl of a mixer with a bread hook. Beat the eggs in the water with the nutmeg, then gradually add this liquid as the mixer turns. Switch to high speed and beat for 3-5 minutes, until the batter is elastic and a little bubbly. Over a large pot of boiling water, use a grater device with large holes to drop in the spaetzle in long, irregular noodles or dumplings. Bring to a boil, then quick-chill spaetzle in water with ice. Repeat process, 2-3 batches, until all batter is cooked.

To Finish:

2 whole saddles venison, trimmed of fat and between ribs to show chops
Thinly sliced chilled pork fat, for "larding"
Salt and freshly ground black pepper
2 tablespoons vegetable oil

For the finished dish, take one of the saddles of venison and "lard" by wrapping in thin sheets of pork fat (slice fat while chilled). Tie with twine and season with salt and pepper. Brown on all sides in the vegetable oil, then transfer to a preheated 450° oven, turning in the pan every 12-15 minutes. Cook for about 45 minutes.

Meanwhile, trim the long tenderloin from the second saddle and slice away all other meat in small cutlets. Using a mallet, pound the cutlets (as with veal scallopine) into thin scallops.

4-5 tablespoons olive oil
1 tablespoon unsalted butter
All-purpose flour
Vegetable oil

When ready to serve, heat 2 tablespoons of the olive oil in a skillet and sear tenderloin on all sides, then set in oven for 5 minutes. Strain the sauce through a fine sieve into a pan over low heat. Sauté the spaetzle in the remaining olive oil until golden and crispy, then stir in the butter. Lightly dust the scallopine with flour and sauté in vegetable oil until browned (they cook quickly, because they are so thin).

Spoon the spaetzle onto heated dinner plates. Slice the tenderloin and serve it around the spaetzle with a chop and a piece of scallopine. Mound red cabbage on the side and spoon on strained sauce. Serves 8-10.

My Grandmother's Chicken

Most cultures around the world find some excuse to cook chicken in close proximity to garlic. Here's chicken the way my grandmother cooked it back on the isle of Capri, a method that actually roasts whole garlic cloves until they're tender and absolutely sweet as you go. Thanks for teaching me this one, Nonna!

⅔ cup pure olive oil
1 whole chicken, cut into serving pieces
½ teaspoon salt
½ teaspoon pepper
8 whole garlic cloves
1 teaspoon chopped fresh rosemary
½ cup white wine
1 tablespoon chopped fresh Italian parsley
Rosemary sprigs

Heat the olive oil in a large skillet. Season the chicken pieces with salt and pepper and brown them on all sides in the hot oil. Set the skillet in a preheated 400° oven until the chicken is crispy, about 30 minutes. Add the garlic and rosemary and return to the oven until the cloves are roasted golden brown. Deglaze the pan by pouring in the wine with the parsley and scraping up browned bits from the bottom. Garnish with sprigs of fresh rosemary. Serves 4-6.

Involtini di Pollo

Italians love to roll things around other things—especially around something salty like ham or bacon and something creamy like cheese, with maybe something green like spinach for good measure. Here is one of the best ways I know to put this love affair with rolling to good effect in your own kitchen.

Sauce:

⅓ cup olive oil
½ cup chopped white onion
1 teaspoon minced garlic
½ cup white wine
2 cups veal demi-glace, homemade or gourmet shop
1 cup heavy cream
¼ teaspoon chopped fresh rosemary
¼ teaspoon salt
¼ teaspoon freshly ground black pepper
1½ cups sliced mushrooms

4 whole chicken breasts, bones removed and lightly pounded out
Salt and freshly ground black pepper
1 cup lightly poached fresh spinach leaves
4 slices prosciutto di Parma
4 slices Fontina cheese
4 leaves fresh basil
½ cup all-purpose flour
2 eggs, beaten
1 cup breadcrumbs, seasoned with salt and pepper
Fresh basil leaves

To prepare the sauce, heat olive oil in a skillet and sauté the onion and garlic until caramelized. Stir in the white wine until it evaporates, then add the demi-glace and bring to a boil. Stir in the cream and reduce to thicken. Add the rosemary, and season with salt and pepper. Turn down the heat and add the mushrooms.

Spread out the chicken breasts on a clean dry surface. Season with salt and pepper. Layer on spinach leaves, prosciutto, cheese and basil. Fold in both sides, then roll from the bottom to the top and secure with a toothpick. Dust each rollup lightly with flour, then dip into the beaten egg and bury in the breadcrumbs. Heat the olive oil in a large skillet. Brown the chicken on all sides in the hot oil, then set the skillet in a preheated 425° oven for 7 minutes, then turn the chicken and cook for 4-5 more minutes, until golden and cooked through. Remove from the oven and let the chicken rest 2-3 minutes before slicing into colorful rounds. Serve the rounds overlapping on dinner plates, with mushrooms and sauce spooned over the top. Serves 4.

Bollito Misto

It gets pretty cold in the winter in the north of Italy, especially in the mountains. That explains this "mixed boil," a super-hearty carnivorous delight that pulls together the best elements of Irish corned beef and cabbage and the equally cold-weather New England "boiled dinner." In my version using beef, pork, chicken and sausage, a certain amount of care goes into cooking some components separately, to make sure each is perfect. I think you'll be happy with the warming results.

½ pound beef inside round, on bone
1 pound lean pork loin, on bone
1 pound pure pork sausage, smoked, or Italian cotechino
1 gallon cool water
4 bay leaves
Salt

Place the beef, pork loin and sausage in a large pot, cover with the water and set over heat. Add the bay leaves and a little salt. Bring to a boil.

1 chicken, cut into serving pieces
½ gallon cool water
3 whole carrots, peeled
1 white onion, peeled and studded with whole cloves
3 stalks celery, roughly chopped
1 whole leek, sliced open and tied with twine
2 whole potatoes, peeled

In a separate pot, boil the chicken in salted water until cooked through. To the first pork-and-sausage bollito, add the onion, carrots, celery, tied leeks and potatoes. As each item becomes cooked, remove it from the boil—carrots, celery and potatoes. When the chicken is cooked, remove it from the broth and pour the broth into the main pot.

1 head cabbage, cored and cut into 8 wedges
Italian fruit mustard (from gourmet shop)

Place the cabbage in a separate pot or deep pan and pour some hot stock over it. Cover with parchment paper and set in a preheated 400° oven to braise the cabbage until it's tender, 20-25 minutes. Remove the bollito from the heat and return the chicken, pork and sausage to the broth with the beef. When cabbage is done, pour that cooking liquid back in as well.

To serve, slice the beef and pork into 8 slices and transfer the pieces to a large bowl, along with the chicken. Cut up and divide the sausage. Add it, with the cabbage wedges and the rest of the vegetables, discarding the twine from the leeks. Ladle the stock over the meats and vegetables. Serve with fruit mustard on the side. Serves 8.

Coniglio Grilletta

Rabbit is a favorite dish in more parts of Europe than I can count—Italy, of course, but also France and Germany and a healthy slice of central Europe. So it's a shame people don't eat rabbit more often here. I hear far too many references to Thumper, or Bugs, or even the Easter Bunny. I'm hoping this rustic wine-kissed stew named after one of my regular customers will help you learn to love rabbit as much as I do.

½ cup vegetable oil
2 rabbits, cut in serving pieces
Freshly squeezed lemon juice
White vinegar
1 teaspoon salt
1 teaspoon freshly ground black pepper
½ cup all-purpose flour
¼ cup pure olive oil
½ cup chopped white onion
1 cup chopped carrot
1 cup chopped celery
1 tablespoon minced garlic
2 tablespoons tomato paste
2 cups red wine

4 cups chicken stock
1 cup chopped Roma tomatoes
1 tablespoon chopped fresh Italian parsley
1 teaspoon chopped fresh rosemary
6 leaves fresh sage, chopped
Hot polenta

Heat the vegetable oil in a deep pan. Wash the rabbit pieces in lemon juice and vinegar, then rinse with cold water. Season with salt and pepper and lightly dust with the flour, shaking off any excess. Brown the rabbit pieces in the hot oil and remove from the pan. Add the olive oil to the drippings and sauté the onion, carrot and celery until caramelized, then stir in the garlic and cook until golden. Add the tomato paste and cook 2-3 minutes, then deglaze with the wine, scraping browned bits from the bottom of the pan.

Add the chicken stock and bring to a boil. Add the tomatoes and herbs and set the pan in a preheated 425° oven until rabbit is tender, about 45 minutes. Serve rabbit and sauce over polenta. Serves 6-8.

Veal Sweetbreads Amaro Dolce

If you think the Chinese wrote the book on the delicate balance of "sweet and sour," then you clearly haven't tasted anything we Italians call *amaro dolce*—which simply reverses the order to be "sour and sweet." As it turns out, it's a perfect way to enjoy these veal sweetbreads with an additional temptation of chanterelle mushrooms.

Poaching Liquid:

2 quarts water
¼ cup white wine
2 bay leaves
2 sage leaves
½ cup chopped leeks
1 cup chopped celery, with leaves
1 quartered onion, studded with whole cloves
1⅓ pounds veal sweetbreads
½ tablespoon salt
½ tablespoon freshly ground black pepper
1 tablespoon all-purpose flour

Bring all the poaching liquid ingredients to a boil, then reduce heat to a simmer for about 5 minutes for the flavors to meld. Poach the sweetbreads until springy, 10-12 minutes, then transfer them to a bowl of cold water with ice to stop the cooking. Reserve the poaching liquid. Peel off as much of the thin skin as possible, being careful not to break the sweetbreads. Slice ¼-inch thick on a bias. Season with salt and pepper. Dust with flour.

Sauce:

2 tablespoons unsalted butter
⅓ cup chopped shallot
1 teaspoon minced garlic
1 tablespoon light brown sugar
2 tablespoons balsamic vinegar
½ pound chanterelle mushrooms, well washed
1 cup stock, strained from poaching
1 cup heavy cream
½ cup white wine
½ teaspoon salt
½ teaspoon freshly ground black pepper
2 leaves fresh sage, chopped
½ teaspoon chopped rosemary
1 tablespoon sliced black truffle (optional)

Prepare the sauce by melting the butter in a large skillet and sautéing the shallot and garlic until caramelized. Stir in the sugar and balsamic vinegar, followed by the chanterelles, tossing to coat thoroughly. Add 1 cup of the poaching liquid, plus the cream and white wine. Season with salt and pepper and reduce by simmering 8-10 minutes. Add the sage, rosemary and black truffle.

2 tablespoons pure olive oil
Fresh sage leaves

Heat the olive oil in a sauté pan and sauté the floured sweetbreads until golden brown. Serve on 4 large dinner plates. Deglaze the sweetbread pan by pouring in the sauce and scraping browned bits from the bottom of the pan. Spoon the chanterelles and sauce over the sweetbreads. Garnish with fresh sage leaves. Serves 4.

Pork Hind Shank Osso Buco

With the popularity of osso buco prepared with veal and lamb, we shouldn't forget what a wonderful meat pork can be too. Here's a classic preparation, with a few different twists and turns. Especially in the north of Italy in the wintertime, every Mamma worth her apron has something like this simmering on the stove.

10 pork hind shanks (1-1¼ pounds each)
1 cup all-purpose flour
2 tablespoons salt
2 tablespoons black pepper
1 cup pure olive oil

Dust the pork shanks with flour and season with the 2 tablespoons of salt and pepper. Brown the meat on all sides in a large pot, in batches if necessary, in the olive oil.

2 medium onions, finely chopped
10 cloves garlic, smashed
1 carrot, finely chopped
3 stalks celery, finely chopped
½ cup tomato paste
2 cups white wine
1 gallon water
1 tablespoon salt
1 tablespoon black pepper
1 teaspoon crushed red pepper

Remove the shanks from the oil and add the onion, garlic, carrot and celery, stirring to pick up browned bits from the pan. Add the tomato paste and stir briefly, then pour in the white wine and water. Season with the remaining salt and pepper and the crushed red pepper. Bring to a boil.

1 tablespoon chopped fresh marjoram
½ teaspoon ground nutmeg
1 whole leek, finely chopped
Leaves from 2 sprigs fresh rosemary, finely chopped

Return the shanks to the pot. Add the fresh herbs and set the pot in a preheated 425° oven, cooking until the meat comes easily off the bone, about 1½ hours. When shanks are tender, remove them from the liquid and set the pot over high heat to boil. Add the leek and rosemary. When sauce is reduced slightly, serve the shanks with the sauce over either Garlic Mashed Potatoes (recipe p. 146) or Spaetzle (recipe p. 157). Serves 10.

Girello d'Agnello in Camicia

Keep your shirt on! That's what we Italians say to this rack of lamb, all dressed up in a "shirt" of breadcrumbs, garlic and herbs. Over the years, this has been a real favorite at Andrea's, with the additional theater of having the rack carved into graceful, perfectly cooked lamb chops right at your table.

2 racks spring lamb, trimmed of excess fat
Salt and freshly ground black pepper
2 sprigs fresh rosemary
8 cloves garlic, halved
¼ cup vegetable oil
Chopped Italian parsley

Season the lamb with salt and pepper. Push the rosemary in beside the bones, then cut small slits and insert the garlic halves. Heat the vegetable oil in a large skillet and brown the racks on all sides, then set the skillet in a preheated 450° oven for about 15 minutes, for medium rare. Remove the racks from the skillet and pour off oil and rendered fat.

Sauce:
¼ cup pure olive oil
1 tablespoon chopped onion
½ teaspoon minced garlic
¼ teaspoon crushed red pepper
¼ cup dry white wine
1 sprig fresh rosemary, chopped
2 leaves fresh mint, chopped
2 sprigs Italian parsley, chopped
⅓ cup butter

In the same skillet, heat the olive oil and sauté the onion, garlic and crushed red pepper until golden. Then add the white wine and bring to a boil, scraping browned bits from the bottom of the pan. Add all remaining sauce ingredients, remove from the heat and whisk in the butter.

Coating:
½ cup dry white wine
2 tablespoons dry mustard
1 cup unseasoned breadcrumbs
Salt and freshly ground black pepper
½ tablespoon minced garlic
2 leaves fresh mint, chopped
2 sprigs Italian parsley, chopped
2 tablespoon pure olive oil

Thoroughly combine all the ingredients and pat the mixture all over the lamb. Return the racks to the oven until the crust is brown, about 10 minutes. Slice the racks into chops (or have your own personal waiter do this tableside!) and serve with the sauce. Garnish with chopped parsley. Serves 4.

Roast Baby Goat

I think it's sad that more people in this country don't enjoy baby goat—or don't think they enjoy it, since most haven't even given it a try. It is, all the same, a delicacy in Italy as well as in many other parts of the world, thanks to its tender meat and mild, wonderful flavors. This recipe is a kind of all-American "pot roast," except with the baby goat where that boring slab of roast beef usually sits.

4 ribs celery
4 cloves garlic
2 tablespoons pure olive oil
2 pounds baby goat meat, trimmed and cut up by butcher
2 cups red wine
2 sprigs fresh mint
2 sprigs fresh rosemary
1 spring fresh oregano
Salt and black pepper to taste
1 pound new potatoes, peeled
2 quarts water

In a roasting pan, sauté the celery and garlic in the olive oil until golden, then add the goat meat and turn until deeply browned on all sides. Add the wine and scrape the browned bits from the bottom of the pan. Add all the herbs and season with salt and pepper. Place pan in a preheated 425° oven for 30 minutes. Add the potatoes and the water and return the pan to the oven for 25-35 minutes, until the meat is tender and the potatoes are cooked. Serve family style on a platter. Garnish with fresh mint or rosemary. Serves 6.

Spezzatino di Vitello Treviso

The wonderful region of the Veneto around Verona, and especially its lovely city of Treviso, gives us this variation of beef stew made with much lighter veal. The technique of making a "spezzatino" is, of course, one that works with almost any type of meat. But the flavors of this dish, like the people of the Veneto, are so special to me that I prepare it their way in their honor.

2 lbs. veal (from round, legs, shoulder), cut bite-sized
Salt and freshly ground black pepper
1 tablespoon all-purpose flour
½ cup pure olive oil
1 cup chopped onion
1 cup chopped carrot
1 cup chopped celery
1 tablespoon minced garlic
1 tablespoon tomato paste
1 cup white wine
6 cups chicken stock
1 teaspoon salt

Season the veal pieces with salt and pepper and dust with flour. Heat about half the olive oil in a large pan or Dutch oven and brown the meat until dark. Remove the veal, add the remaining olive oil and sauté the onion, carrot, celery and garlic until caramelized. Add the tomato paste and cook 2-3 minutes. Add the white wine, scraping up brown bits from the bottom of the pan. Pour in the chicken stock, season with salt and bring to a boil.

1 teaspoon chopped fresh sage
1 teaspoon chopped fresh rosemary
2 bay leaves

Return the veal to the stew, along with the sage, rosemary and bay leaves. Set the pot in a pre-heated 425° oven until the veal is tender, about 45 minutes.

8 black olives
1 cup sliced mushrooms
1 cup chopped red bell peppers
1 cup chopped green bell peppers

Using your fingers, crush the olives above the stew and add them near the end of the cooking time. For maximum color, briefly sauté the mushrooms and bell peppers in a little olive oil in a separate pan. Add these to the stew when it comes out of the oven.

6 cups cooked fettuccine
½ cup melted butter
½ cup water from pasta
Grated Parmesan cheese
Italian parsley leaves

Toss the cooked fettuccine with the butter. Add the pasta water into the stew. Serve the stew over the fettuccine, sprinkled with Parmesan cheese. Garnish with parsley leaves. Serves 6-8.

Bistecca alla Fiorentina

It should tell you something about this dish (and possibly about the Florentines) that they usually call this by only its first name—"Bistecca"—and figure everyone will know which steak they mean. Or else, they call it "bistecca al sangue," which means something like "bloody steak." Florentines didn't rule commerce, politics and the arts during the Renaissance by stocking up on tofu! Fact is, they love this huge hunk of porterhouse barely passed through the general neighborhood of heat. Dining among the people of Florence, you'd do well to follow their lead, if you dare. In the privacy of your own home, you can fudge a little toward medium rare or even medium.

1 (2-pound) porterhouse steak

Grill the steak on both sides just long enough to create grill marks, then transfer it on a broiling pan into a preheated 450° oven. Broil no more than about 10 minutes.

Sauce:
1 cup extra-virgin olive oil
1 tablespoon minced garlic
1 tablespoon chopped fresh Italian parsley
1 teaspoon finely chopped green onion
⅛ teaspoon salt
⅛ teaspoon black pepper
Juice of 1 lemon

Meanwhile, prepare the sauce by mixing all ingredients in a bowl.

Fresh spinach leaves, wilted in hot water and patted dry

Place spinach leaves on the plates and lay the steak atop them. Ladle the sauce over steak and spinach. Serves 2.

Peppercorn Beef Filet Thomas

In that great, centuries-long borrowing over the back fence that was the history of Italian and French cuisines, you might know this dish elsewhere as *steak au poivre*. It doesn't really matter what you call it as much as how much you love it!

2 (9-10 ounce) beef filets
½ teaspoon salt
½ cup whole black peppercorns, or mixture of black, green and red
¼ cup vegetable oil

1 tablespoon pure olive oil
1 teaspoon minced garlic
4 cups fresh baby spinach leaves
1 tablespoon water
Salt and black pepper to taste
¼ teaspoon crushed red pepper

1 teaspoon minced garlic
½ teaspoon finely chopped French shallot
1 tablespoon cognac or other brandy
⅓ cup heavy cream
¼ cup red wine
1 tablespoon unsalted butter

Salt the filets and coat with black peppercorns, pressing them into the surface with your hands. Heat the vegetable oil in an ovenproof skillet and sear the meat on each side, then transfer the skillet to a preheated 450° oven for 8-10 minutes.

Meanwhile, in a sauté pan, heat the olive oil and caramelize the garlic until golden. Stir in the spinach leaves until wilted by the heat, then add the water. Season to taste with salt and pepper, then add the red pepper.

When filets are done, remove them from the skillet and pour off the excess oil. Heat quickly and stir in the garlic and shallots. Stir to caramelize, then deglaze the pan with the cognac. Add the heavy cream and red wine, reducing slightly over high heat. Add the butter and incorporate. Serve the filets topped by plenty of the sauce. Serves 2.

Veal Scallopine Don Federico

Everybody loves veal Marsala. In fact, people love it so much they eat the sauce with chicken, fish or just about anything else. Here's my take on veal Marsala, which pays tribute to one Italian classic while flirting unexpectedly with another—a dish you'll sometimes hear called Saltimbocca.

2 tablespoons olive oil
4 (4-oz.) veal "scallops," cut from the leg, pounded thin
All-purpose flour
½ teaspoon minced garlic
⅓ cup Marsala wine
⅓ cup white wine

Heat the olive oil in a pan. Lightly sprinkle the veal with flour. Brown in the hot oil, only about 2 minutes per side. Remove the scallops. In the pan, caramelize the garlic until golden, then deglaze with Marsala and white wine, stirring to scrape up the browned bits.

4 slices prosciutto
4 slices Fontina cheese
Grated Parmesan cheese

Set the veal slices on a pan and top each with a slice of prosciutto, a slice of Fontina and a sprinkle of Parmesan. Set in a preheated 350° oven for 5 minutes, until heated through and cheese has melted.

⅓ cup unsalted butter
¼ teaspoon ground sage
Salt to taste
¼ teaspoon chopped fresh Italian parsley

Meanwhile, complete the sauce by melting the butter in the pan and stirring in the sage, along with salt to taste (be careful—most prosciutto is salty) and parsley. Serve 2 slices of veal per person, with the sauce spooned over the top. Serves 2.

Veal Chop Jill

This summer dish is named after the daughter of two great friends of mine, Sidney and Marilyn Lassen—someone I watched grow up during her visits to my dining room. You'll be amazed by how light and healthy this feels on a hot day, whether you are in New Orleans or Calabria.

2 (12-14 ounce) veal chops, on the bone
½ cup all-purpose flour
Salt and black pepper
⅓ cup vegetable oil
2 cups arugula
Lemon halves

Sauce:
3 Roma tomatoes, roughly chopped
⅓ cup extra-virgin olive oil
⅓ cup capers
⅓ cup white wine
¼ cup red onion
1 tablespoon chopped fresh basil
1 tablespoon chopped fresh oregano
1 tablespoon chopped fresh Italian parsley
½ teaspoon salt
¼ teaspoon crushed red pepper
Juice of 1 lemon

Slicing down with a knife, butterfly the chops. Spread the "wings" on either side and pound out until very thin. Coat with flour, shaking off any excess, and season with salt and pepper. Heat the vegetable oil in a skillet and spread out each veal chop to brown, turning once, about 3 minutes in all. Set on a baking sheet and finish cooking in a preheated 425° oven, 10-12 minutes.

Meanwhile, prepare the uncooked sauce by combining all ingredients in a mixing bowl. To serve, top each veal chop with arugula and then spoon on the sauce. Garnish with lemon halves and drizzle with olive oil. Serves 2.

My favorite pergolato, Antonio & Maria's place

Dolci

Poached Peaches with Mascarpone Cream

We can thank the popularity of the Bellini champagne cocktail for showing the world just how much we Italians love our fresh peaches. Summertime is peach season where I cook now, and that means it's time we added the following dessert to all of our menus. It is super!

Peaches:

1 quart water
1 quart red wine
1 cinnamon stick
2 whole cloves
8 peeled peaches
½ cup sugar
1 tablespoon cornstarch

Heat the water, wine, cinnamon and cloves just until boiling, then lower heat and poach the peaches for 20 minutes. Remove the peaches and set in refrigerator to chill. Prepare the sauce by heating 2 cups of the poaching liquid with the sugar. Dissolve the cornstarch in a bit of the sauce, then add it in to thicken. Set bowl of sauce in the refrigerator to chill.

Mascarpone Cream:

2 cups heavy cream
1 cup mascarpone cheese
¼ cup powdered sugar
¼ cup granulated sugar
1 egg yolk
¼ cup peach liqueur

When ready to serve, whip the cream until frothy, then fold in the mascarpone along with the sugars, egg yolk and peach liqueur. Slice the peaches in half with a serrated knife and remove the pit. Thinly slice each peach. Spoon sauce generously onto 8 dessert plates, fan out peach slices atop each pool and spoon the whipped cream into the center. Garnish with fresh mint leaves. Serves 8.

Fig Tart la Guardia

One of the great contributions of classical cuisine is the delicate and delicious fruit tart. We Italians love any fresh, seasonal fruit—but fresh figs make one of the best tarts you'll ever taste.

Pastry Cream:
2 quarts milk
6 ounces cornstarch
5 eggs
¼ pound unsalted butter
1 pound sugar
1 tablespoon vanilla extract

Prepare the pastry cream by mixing 2 cups of milk with the cornstarch and eggs. In a saucepan over high heat, mix the remaining milk with the butter and sugar. When it is boiling, add the first mixture along with the vanilla. Return to a boil and remove from the heat. For sanitation reasons, it is important to cool the pastry cream as quickly as possible. We recommend pouring it out on a sheet pan, covering it with plastic wrap and setting it in the refrigerator.

Crust:
½ pound butter
1 cup sugar
3 eggs, lightly beaten
3½ cups all-purpose flour

Cream the butter and sugar together in a stand-up mixer, then gradually add the eggs, scraping down the sides of the bowl with a spatula. Add the flour a little at a time to form a soft dough. Wrap the dough and let it rest in the refrigerator 3-4 hours. Once it is rested, knead the dough and roll it out about an eighth-inch thick. Lay it into a tart pan and trim off the edges. Cover with parchment paper and some weight (such as dry beans) to keep it down. Bake in a preheated 350° oven until golden, about 10 minutes. Let crust cool.

Tart:
⅔ cup high-quality fig preserves
1 tablespoon Triple Sec
1 teaspoon vanilla extract
10 fresh figs, sliced
Powdered sugar
Additional sliced figs
Fresh mint leaves

Spread the crust with the fig preserves. Combine 2 cups of pastry cream with the Triple Sec and vanilla, then spread generously over the preserves. Layer the entire area with sliced figs. Press down gently.

Glaze:
1 cup water
1½ tablespoons Triple Sec
½ cup sugar
2 tablespoons cornstarch

Combine all ingredients in a saucepan, heat until bubbly and then simmer until thick. Brush on the glaze. Sprinkle with powdered sugar. Decorate plate with additional sliced figs and fresh mint leaves. Serves 10.

Lemon Crostata Peter

Here's a light Italian rendition of a lemon tart. All the beating of the filling makes for a frothy, almost airy consistency, instead of the heavier one associated with lemon cream pies.

Crust:

1 stick unsalted butter
2 cups all-purpose flour
½ teaspoon salt
1 egg, beaten

In a mixing bowl, combine the butter with the flour and salt, using your hands or a pastry cutter. Add the egg, kneading it in. Wrap the dough in plastic and refrigerate for 10 minutes.

Filling:

4 eggs
¾ cup sugar
Zest of 2 lemons
Juice of 1 lemon
4 tablespoons butter, melted

In a standing mixer, or using a hand mixer, combine the eggs, sugar and lemon zest. Beat on high until light and frothy, about 3 minutes. Add the lemon juice and melted butter, beating at a lower speed for 1 minute.

Flour
Butter
Powdered sugar

Butter and flour an 8-inch tart pan, shaking off excess. Place the dough in the center of the pan and spread with your fingers to form a thin, even layer. Pour in the lemon filling and bake in a preheated 350° oven until cooked through and light brown on top, 25-35 minutes. Let the crostata cool. Dust with powdered sugar. Serves 6.

Tiramisu   I was happy to be the chef who introduced this relatively new Italian dessert to New Orleans. While most recipes you see for the original use those dry ladyfingers, we decided our guests would be happier if we used fresh sponge cake. The whole dessert comes off moister and lighter as a result.

2 egg yolks *¼ cup sugar* *1 cup mascarpone cheese*	In a bowl, whisk the egg yolks with ¼ cup sugar, then fold in the mascarpone.
1 pint heavy cream, chilled *¼ cup sugar* *1 teaspoon vanilla extract*	Whip the cream in a separate bowl with ¼ cup sugar and the vanilla until almost stiff. Combine the two mixtures and whip until stiff peaks form.
¼ cup sugar *2 tablespoons water* *¾ cup espresso or strong brewed coffee* *1 ounce rum*	Prepare a syrup by dissolving the sugar into the water, coffee and rum.
1 sponge cake, sliced into 3 layers *2 tablespoons cocoa powder*	Brush the coffee-rum liquid over a layer of the cake, then smooth on a half inch of the mascarpone cream. Brush the second layer with the coffee-rum liquid and set that side down atop the mascarpone cream. Brush the top of that with the liquid, then spread on another half inch of the mascarpone cream. Repeat with the remaining layer. Cover the top and sides of the cake with mascarpone cream. Sprinkle the top of the cake with cocoa powder. Refrigerate at least 3 hours. Serves 8-10.

Torta Caprese   I remember when this idea first started making the rounds as a "new dessert" aimed at Americans who consider themselves "chocoholics." Of course, there have been chocoholics since the Aztecs invented the stuff and the Spanish conquistadors took some home to Europe. Chocolate has been a fascination ever since, and always will be.

2 sticks unsalted butter
All-purpose flour
4 eggs, yolks and whites separated
5 ounces bittersweet chocolate
1½ cups blanched almonds, finely ground

Butter a 10-inch round cake pan with 1 tablespoon of butter. Dust with flour, shaking off excess. Beat the egg yolks in one bowl with the sugar, and beat the whites in a second bowl until soft peaks form. Fold the whites into the yolk mixture to form a frothy batter. Combine the chocolate with the remaining butter in the top of a double boiler over medium-low heat, stirring until melted. Fold the ground almonds into the batter, followed by the chocolate and melted butter. Pour this into the prepared pan and bake in a preheated 350° oven for 30 minutes. Set aside to cool.

Powdered sugar
Fresh raspberries and blueberries

Dust with powdered sugar and garnish with fresh berries. Slice and serve. Serves 12.

Torta alle Fragole Abbie

In this country, few things say summer better than strawberry shortcake, usually nothing more than the season's freshest, reddest strawberries atop cake with a spoonful of whipped cream on top. In Italy, we turn the same basic construction into this glorious summer "torta."

1 pint strawberries

Slice the strawberries, saving the tops to use as garnish.

¾ cup freshly whipped cream
1 cup Pastry Cream (recipe p. 185)
½ cup mascarpone cheese
¼ cup Triple Sec
¼ cup Grand Marnier

Prepare a frosting by whipping together the whipped cream, pastry cream, mascarpone, Triple Sec and Grand Marnier.

½ cup sugar
¼ cup warm water
1 sponge cake, cut into 3 layers

Make a syrup by dissolving the sugar in warm water and brush this onto a layer of cake, followed by ½ inch of the frosting. Top with a generous layer of sliced strawberries. Repeat the sequence on each layer of cake, assembling as you go. Smooth the frosting around the sides and top. Use the strawberry tops to decorate. Chill. Serves 8-10.

Zuppa Inglese Rosario

Don't get confused: this so-called "English soup" is actually a wonderful dessert that most closely resembles what the English call trifle. It's a lovely layered affair of fresh fruit, cake and liqueur. And … it's a light and summery way to end a great meal.

1 9-inch sponge cake
1 cup kirschwasser or other cherry liqueur
3 cups Pastry Cream (see recipe p. 185)
3 cups fresh strawberries, sliced
3 bananas, sliced
3 cups whipped cream
½ cup candied fruit
1 cup crushed pistachio nuts

Moisten the sponge cake with kirschwasser and set it into the bottom of a one-gallon bowl. Layer this, in order, with pastry cream, strawberries, bananas, whipped cream, candied fruit and pistachios, then repeat the sequence. Top with whipped cream with candied fruits and pistachios. Chill the bowl in the refrigerator. Slice in front of your guests. Serves 12.

Budino Caramellata This simple dessert, called *crema caramellata* in Italy and, of course, *flan* in Spain and the Spanish Americas, is a favorite at Andrea's. Sometimes you'll hear it called cup custard around New Orleans as well. It isn't hard to make. It is hard to stop eating.

Caramel:
1 cup sugar
¼ cup water
⅛ teaspoon cream of tartar

Dissolve the sugar in the water with the cream of tartar. Carefully bring this "slurry" to a boil, then lower the heat and simmer until the center is light brown. Quickly pour the caramel into the bottoms of 8 custard cups.

Custard:
1 quart whole milk
1 pound sugar
10 eggs
1 tablespoon pure vanilla extract

Make the custard by combining all ingredients in the bowl of a mixer and beat on slow speed for 5 minutes. Strain into the custard cups atop the sauce. Set the cups into a baking pan of hot water and let the temperature rise, then set pan in a pre-heated 325° oven. Bake for about 30 minutes, until the custard is set and the tops are lightly browned. Remove from the oven and let cool for 15 minutes. Refrigerate until ready to serve. Serves 8.

Cannoli Palermitani

With its rich Sicilian-American tradition, New Orleans has inhaled lots more than its share of cannoli over the generations. The sweet treats are, naturally, sold ready-made—but those can't replace the good feeling (and great taste!) you get by making your own.

Shells:

1½ cups all-purpose flour
5 tablespoons Marsala wine
1 tablespoon sugar
⅛ teaspoon cocoa powder
⅛ teaspoon ground cinnamon
⅛ teaspoon salt
Vegetable oil for frying

Mix all ingredients except the oil in a ball, kneading with your fingers until the batter forms a gritty ball. Roll it out on a board. Run the batter through a pasta machine, starting at thickest setting (No. 1) and ending at No. 6, about the thickness of a lasagna noodle. Cut 4-inch-wide discs with a cookie cutter or sharp knife. Wrap these around cannoli forms and fry in oil preheated to 375°. Remove the forms and let the shells cool.

Filling:

1 pound ricotta cheese
1 cup sugar
½ cup candied fruit, chopped small
2 tablespoons chocolate chips
1 tablespoon vanilla extract
½ ounce Triple Sec liqueur

Mix all ingredients in another bowl. Use a pastry bag to fill the cooled shells.

Crushed pistachio nuts
Powdered sugar

Dip the end in pistachios and dust with powdered sugar. Makes 20-24 cannoli.

Orancia Panna Cotta

This classic Italian dessert, whose name means nothing more than "cooked cream," for a long time took a back seat in this country to things like crème brûlée, or even the Italian tiramisu that our guests have loved so much. In the past few years, though, we've had more and more guests asking for panna cotta. And this recipe should show you why.

2 cups whole milk
2 cups heavy cream
1 tablespoon powdered gelatin (or 3 sheets)
2 teaspoons vanilla extract
1 teaspoon orange flower water
Zest of 1 orange
Fresh berries
Orange slices

Pour the milk into a mixing bowl. Heat the cream in a pan. Placing the bowl over a hot water bath, dissolve the gelatin in the milk. Add the vanilla, orange flower water and orange zest to the cream, just until lukewarm. Pour the warmed milk into the cream. Ladle the mixture into serving bowls and chill in the refrigerator until firm, 4-5 hours. Serve garnished with fresh berries of the season and orange slices. Serves 4.

Note: The wonderful thing about panna cotta is its adaptability. To give this version a little extra punch, you can always add 1 tablespoon of Grand Marnier. Or you can make it any flavor you want.

Crespelle Marilyn Lassen

The crêpe is one of those wonderful things that work as a savory dish, as in Crespelle di Formaggio, or as a dessert, as in this treat named after the wife of one of my best friends in New Orleans, Sidney Lassen. In the tradition of the oh-so-French crêpes Suzettes, I like to keep things bright with citrus; but there's tons of freedom for you to experiment with different flavors on your own.

1 cup dairy sour cream
1 cup mascarpone cheese
1 cup cream cheese
½ cup confectioners sugar
¼ cup granulated sugar
½ cup Triple Sec liqueur
1 teaspoon orange flower water
Zest from 1 orange
Zest from 1 lemon

Prepare the filling in a mixing bowl by combining all ingredients until smooth. Refrigerate.

Sauce:
2 cups water
Juice of 1 orange
Juice of 1 lemon
½ cup granulated sugar
2 cups strawberries or other seasonal berries, trimmed and cut
1 tablespoon cornstarch dissolved in 1 tablespoon water

Prepare the sauce by heating the water, citrus juices, sugar and berries to a boil, then simmering for 10 minutes. Stir in the dissolved cornstarch. Remove from heat when the sauce thickens.

20 prepared crêpes
Confectioners sugar
Fresh mint leaves

To complete the dish, spoon about 1 tablespoon of the filling into the center of each crêpe. Fold in the ends, then roll gently to close. Place the folded crêpes in a baking pan lightly brushed with butter. Heat in a preheated 375° oven for about 8 minutes. Serve topped with strawberry sauce, dusted with confectioners sugar and garnished with fresh mint leaves. Serves 10.

Chocolate Crème Brûlée

Over the past decade or so, crème brûlée has become one of the most popular desserts on any restaurant's menu—a testament to the sensory wonderfulness of a smooth, lush custard beneath a crispy topping of "burnt" sugar. Crème brûlée alone accounts for the number of small blowtorches sold these days in cookware stores all over America.

1 quart whipping cream	Bring the whipping cream to a boil and remove from heat.
8 egg yolks *½ cup sugar* *1 tablespoon vanilla* *½ cup cocoa powder*	In a stainless steel bowl, mix the egg yolks and sugar with a whisk. Add the vanilla extract. Carefully add the whipped cream to the egg yolk mixture. Whisk in the chocolate powder a little at a time. Mix very well.
1 quart water	Divide the mixture evenly into 7 crème brulé dishes. Place a sheet pan on a rack in the oven and slowly pour the water into it. Place all of the dishes in the pan. Bake at 400° for 30 minutes. Allow to cool.
¼ cup brown sugar *in-the-raw*	Sprinkle brown sugar evenly over each dish. Using a torch, caramelize the top until it is brown in color. Serves 7.

Torta Felice

Here is a favorite Italian cake for any holiday, one perhaps known best as Pastiera during the Easter season but terrific for Christmas and other times as well. That's why we call it "Happy Torte"! It is quite different in texture from many familiar cakes and other desserts, with its wheat berries and absence of any flour. Still, if you notice the candied fruit and think it's that same old holiday fruitcake they give you at the office every year—think again!

1 cup whole wheat berries 1 gallon water	Soak the wheat berries in the water overnight, then boil until tender, 1-2 hours.
2 cups ricotta cheese 2 tablespoons orange flower water 1 tablespoon vanilla extract 4 egg yolks, lightly beaten 1 teaspoon ground cinnamon 1 tablespoon Marsala wine ½ cup candied fruit 2 tablespoons confectioners sugar 2 tablespoons granulated sugar Zest of 1 orange Zest of 1 lemon 4 egg whites	In a mixing bowl, prepare the batter by combining the ricotta, orange flower water, vanilla, egg yolks, cinnamon, wine, fruit, sugars and zests. With an electric mixer or a hand whisk, beat the egg whites until stiff peaks form, then fold them into the batter.
2 prepared pie crusts 1 extra pie crust pastry for covering 1 egg, beaten	Pour into the pie crusts. Cut the extra pastry into long strips and lay across the top of the batter in a thatch pattern. Brush with the egg and bake in a preheated 400° oven until golden brown, about 45 minutes. Let cool 10 minutes before slicing. Serves 6-8.

My isle of Capri

Index of Recipes

Index of Recipes

❦ ❦ ❦

The Parents

At home in Capri with the family

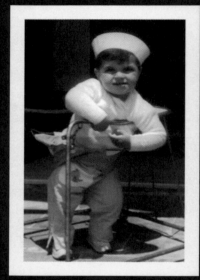

The future Chef

The early "competetion"